# Writing Skills, Grade 7
## Contents

# Introduction

Language expression is an important skill for students to master. Learning to write helps students to interact with the larger world. It helps them to construct personal meaning and to communicate personal experiences. Writing well is the foundation for success in most school subjects.

One way to learn to write better is through imitation. *Writing Skills* gives students practice in reading and writing different types of papers. Students read original papers written by experienced writers, respond to what they read, analyze what they read, plan and organize writing ideas, write and revise drafts, and practice self-assessment. In addition, students have the opportunities to apply instructional standards, refresh their writing and language skills, build their confidence as writers, and prepare for standardized writing tests.

## Standards for English Language Arts

The National Council of Teachers of English (NCTE) has stressed that "all students must have the opportunities and resources to develop the language skills they need to pursue life's goals and to participate fully as informed, productive members of society." The NCTE also states that students need to "apply a wide range of strategies as they write and use different writing process elements appropriately to communicate with different audiences for a variety of purposes." This book helps students to practice a variety of writing strategies. To learn more about the NCTE's twelve standards for the development of creative and innovative Language Arts curricula and instruction, visit **http://www.ncte.org/standards/**.

## Organization

The book is divided into nine units. Each unit deals with a different type of writing. Each unit has seven parts. First, students read a Model Paper. Then, they Respond to the Model Paper. Next, they Analyze the Model Paper. After they have studied the model paper, they begin the process of writing their own paper. They receive a Writing Assignment, which includes a graphic organizer. A page is provided for the students to begin their First Draft. Once the first draft is complete, they begin to Revise the Draft. Then, they evaluate their own work or that of a classmate using a Writing Report Card.

## Diagnostic Writing Prompt and Sample Papers

When you begin a writing program with your class, an informal assessment of students' writing skills helps you determine their initial strengths and weaknesses. Use the narrative prompt below to obtain diagnostic anchor papers for your class. Evaluate these papers using the Scoring Rubric on page 4. Before you begin the evaluation process, you may want to examine the sample papers and commentaries (pages 6–15). The papers are examples of student writing at each level of the rubric. The commentaries provide explanations of why each paper received its rating. All the sample papers are assigned a value from 4 to 1 using the Scoring Rubric on page 4.

Ask students to discuss or use their own paper to respond to the following questions:
1. What is the best thing that has ever happened to you?
2. When and where did it happen?
3. What made it so special?

Then, read the following directions aloud: *Write a story describing the best thing that ever happened to you. Give details that help your readers to imagine the story you tell.*

Encourage students to plan before writing their narrative. Suggest that they list the main ideas they will write about. Tell them to put the main ideas in the order they will write about them. Remind students to give details that support each main idea.

## Proofreading Symbols

A chart of proofreading symbols is included on page 16. Students are encouraged to use these symbols as they edit and revise drafts. You may want to post the proofreading symbols as a ready reference for students.

## Scoring Student Writing

Many states now include writing assessments in their statewide testing programs. The evaluation of these assessments often relies upon a state-specific scoring rubric. You may use your state's scoring rubric to evaluate your students' writing performance and progress. If your state does not provide a rubric, you may use the 4-point Scoring Rubric on page 4 that was used to evaluate the sample papers provided in this book. Still another option is the *6 + 1 Traits™ of Analytic Writing Assessment Scoring Guide.* This guide and sample student papers that have been evaluated using this guide can be found at **http://www.nwrel.org/assessment/**.

## Writing Conference Record

A Writing Conference Record can be found on page 5. Questions and directions in the record help you evaluate each student's writing process skills and determine performance objectives. Records are used within the context of student-teacher conferences. Conferences promote dialogue about the writing experience and prompt discussion of ideas for writing, critical analysis, and opportunities for reading aloud. Conferences also help distinguish writing as a purposeful and rewarding activity.

## Additional Writing Prompts

Additional writing prompts for each kind of writing are included below. These prompts can be used to give students additional writing practice in one or more kinds of writing. They can also be used as reinforcement in other instructional settings, in learning centers, and for homework. Encourage students to use writing plans to organize their thoughts and notes before writing a draft.

## Personal Narrative

1. You make decisions every day, some small, some large. Think about an important decision that you've had to make. How did you make the decision? How was your life different after you made the decision? What might have happened if you'd made another choice? Write a story about your decision and how it affected your life.

2. Which birthday has meant the most to you? Write a narrative that explains why this birthday was your favorite. Include dialogue to add dimension to the characters in your narrative.

3. Think of the worst thing that ever happened to you. When did it happen? Where were you? What made it so awful? Write a story describing the worst thing that ever happened to you. Be sure to include details that help your readers picture the events in the story.

4. Courage comes in many forms. There is physical courage, as when a person helps someone in a dangerous situation. And there is moral courage, when you do something that you know is right, even when it's hard. Think of a time that you were courageous. What happened? What did you do? What made you act? What was the result? Write a story describing this event. Include vivid details that make your story come alive.

## Descriptive Story

1. Look through the real estate ads in your local paper. Find an ad that interests you. Imagine the house and the people who are selling it. What is the house like? What are the people like? Why are they selling the house? Write a story describing the house and why it is for sale. Remember to use descriptions based on your five senses.

2. Did you have a favorite toy as a child? When did you get it? What kinds of games did you play with the toy? What happened to the toy? Think about your childhood treasure. Write a descriptive story about you and your toy. Include vivid details that help the reader picture the toy and the time you spent playing with it.

3. Imagine that you could visit any planet in the universe. Where would you go? What would you do there? Write a story about your adventure. Involve all the senses in your descriptions. Use similes and metaphors in your writing.

4. Imagine you are camping in a forested area. The sun is shining through the trees, but a summer storm is on the way. Make notes about what you see, hear, feel, smell, and taste as you wait for the storm. Write a story using this setting.

## How-to Paper

1. Everyone knows that middle school is different from elementary school. Help new sixth-graders by writing a paper telling them how to prepare for middle school.

2. Tests. You can't get away from them. But there are ways that you can get ready for tests. Jot down all the things that you can do to prepare for a test. Then, interview your classmates and teachers for additional ideas. Finally, write a paper describing how to study for a test.

3. You probably celebrate several holidays during the year. Think of your favorite holiday and all the traditions and decorations that accompany it. Then, write a paper describing how to celebrate this holiday.

4. Imagine that you are baby-sitting a four-year-old and you need to teach him or her how to tie his or her shoestrings. Write a how-to paper describing this process. Include illustrations so the child can follow along.

## Compare and Contrast Paper

1. Think about the music you like to listen to. How is it like the music that your parents enjoy? How is it different? Write a paper that compares and contrasts the two types of music.

2. What are your two favorite TV shows? The next time you watch the shows, take notes about the characters, plots, and settings. Then, write a paper that tells how the two shows are alike and how they are different.

3. Think about a character in one of your favorite books. What does he or she like to do? What is he or she good at? What kinds of problems does he or she have to overcome? Write a paper that compares and contrasts this character with yourself.

4. Although insects outnumber people, we often try to ignore the creepy crawly creatures. Choose two insects. Think about what you would like to learn about them. Then, use your library, the Internet, and other resources to learn more about the insects. Write a paper that compares and contrasts these two insects.

## Short Report

1. Your house is full of things that you use every day. Pick one object to research. When was it invented? How is it manufactured? Does it have any other uses? Write a report about this object.

2. Money can't buy you love, but it does buy many other things that you want or need. Research the history of money. Then, write a report telling how money has changed over time.

3. Do you know how and when your state joined the United States? Who helped shape your state into the wonderful place it is today? Research your state's history and share it with others in a short report.

4. Everyone has heard of Thomas Edison and Benjamin Franklin, but what about the millions of other inventors who have changed our world? Use your library, the Internet, and other resources to learn about inventors such as Grace Hopper and Elijah McCoy. Then, write a short report so others can learn about them, too.

## Persuasive Writing

1. Many people believe that everyone should learn at least one language other than English. What is your opinion? Should students be required to learn a foreign language in order to graduate from high school? Write a persuasive letter to your principal stating your opinion. Be sure to support your opinion with examples and details.

2. Think about your favorite game or sport. What makes it so special? Write a persuasive essay to convince your friends to play the game.

3. Have you seen a movie recently that didn't live up to all the hype? What made it so bad? Write a movie review persuading others not to see the movie. Support your opinion with examples and details from the movie.

4. Your mom just got a wonderful job offer, but the job is in another city. Your family is discussing whether to move or to stay where you are. What would you like to do? Write a letter to persuade your family to see things your way.

5. The school board is considering buying uniforms for everyone at your school. They say wearing uniforms will help students concentrate on their studies. What is your opinion? Write a persuasive essay for the school newspaper to convince others that your opinion is the right one.

# Scoring Rubric for Writing

## Score of 4
### The student's response ...

- <u>clearly and completely</u> addresses the writing task,

- demonstrates an understanding of the purpose for writing,

- maintains a single focus,

- presents a central idea supported by relevant details and explanations,

- uses paragraphs to organize main ideas and supporting details under the umbrella of the central idea,

- presents content in a logical order or sequence,

- uses variety in sentence types and lengths,

- uses language appropriate to the writing task, such as language rich with sensory details in a model of descriptive writing,

- summarizes main ideas in a concluding paragraph in a model of expository or persuasive writing,

- establishes and defends a position in a model of persuasive writing, and

- has few or no errors in the standard rules of English grammar, punctuation, capitalization, and spelling.

## Score of 3
### The student's response ...

- <u>generally</u> follows the criteria described above, and

- has some errors in the standard rules of English grammar, punctuation, capitalization, and spelling, but not so many that a reader's comprehension is impaired.

## Score of 2
### The student's response ...

- <u>marginally</u> follows the criteria described above, and

- has several errors in the standard rules of English grammar, punctuation, capitalization, and spelling that may impair a reader's comprehension.

## Score of 1
### The student's response ...

- <u>fails</u> to follow the criteria described above, and

- has numerous and serious errors in the standard rules of English grammar, punctuation, capitalization, and spelling that impair a reader's comprehension.

# Writing Conference Record

Encourage each student to share a writing sample with you. Then complete the conference record below. Invite each student to participate in several writing conferences. Use the records to assess each student's skills and progress.

Student's Name _____ Date _____

Title of the Writing Sample discussed today: _____

## Kind of writing this sample represents:

☐ Personal Narrative    ☐ How-to Paper    ☐ Persuasive Letter

☐ Narrative    ☐ Compare and Contrast Paper    ☐ Persuasive Movie Review

☐ Descriptive Story    ☐ Short Report    ☐ Persuasive Essay

| Questions or Directions | Student's Responses and Teacher's Notes |
|---|---|
| What were your writing goals for this paper? | |
| Why did you choose this kind of writing? | |
| Why did you choose this topic? | |
| How did you organize your ideas and notes for this paper? | |
| Describe the writing process you used to write this paper, including revising your draft. | |
| What do you like most about this paper? | |
| In general, what is your strongest writing skill? | |
| Which writing skill do you think you need to improve? How will you do it? | |

Date of next writing conference: _____

# Diagnostic Sample Narratives

The following sample represents a narrative that meets the criteria for a 4-point paper.

## The Best Thing Ever!

My mom is in the military. When Mom left for a six-month tour of duty I had to stay with my uncle. I really missed my mom, but there wasn't much I could do about it. One night I was sitting on the couch watching television when my uncle said, "Guess what! In one month you're going to take a plane to see your mother in Hawaii." I leapt off the couch in excitement and ran upstairs to my room. I jumped on my bed, giggling and talking to myself all evening.

On September 7, my uncle and I went to the airport. There were kids everywhere. Some were in line, but most of them were running around and chattering like monkeys. Once we got our tickets, we were packed into a little, hot waiting room. I was sweating and breathing heavily as I waited for my turn to board the plane. Finally we were allowed on the plane and it took off. Eight hours later we landed and I got to see my mom! When she saw me, she gasped and I gave her a huge hug. She put a lei around my neck. A lei is a necklace made of real flowers. It was amazing and beautiful. We picked up my bags, then made our way to the ship. We found the den where we would sleep and I put my stuff away. We wanted to get an early start on our special day.

The next morning we woke up at six o'clock am. We started our day climbing Diamond Head Volcano. That might sound like fun to you, but just looking at the mountain made me exhausted! It was a very tiring climb, but once we got to the top it was all worth it. We could see the whole, lush green island!

Next we went snorkeling. We put on masks with snorkles and wore flippers on our feet. Mom and I laughed at each other, because we looked like alien space creatures. In a way we were, because the equipment let us enter another world under the water. I saw a lot of beautifully colored fish, and even got to pet a few.

This wonderful day ended with a luau. We watched as several people dug up a pig that had been cooking since 5:00 a.m. It was so cool—that was going to be our dinner! That pig was delicious. After dinner, men and women hula dancers put on a show. Women were cheering and whistling for the men dancers, and men were staring and drooling as they watched the women dance. The hula dancers even showed people how to do the hula. It was funny, like Comic View.

I have wanted to go to Hawaii ever since I was in second grade, so this was a dream come true. The thing that made this day most special, though, was spending time with my mom. We finally had a chance to bond, something we've needed ever since my dad left four years ago. I will treasure this memory and share it with my kids when I have some.

## Commentary

This student has a clear understanding of the purpose for writing and has addressed the writing prompt completely. Relevant details and vivid descriptions, major strengths in this paper, help the reader picture the events of the writer's special day. The writer's enthusiasm and excitement shine through the essay and are especially effective in drawing the reader into the narrative.

This narrative has a clear, consistent organizational structure. In addition, the student obviously demonstrates mastery of the conventions of English. The few errors that are present do not impede the reader's understanding of the narrative. A variety of sentence types is included, making the paper more interesting to read. The conclusion solidifies the essay, clearly summarizing the reasons that this day was the best thing that ever happened to the writer.

*(Go on to the next page.)*

The following sample represents a narrative that meets the criteria for a 3-point paper.

## Winning the Nationals

The best thing that ever happened to me was when my softball team won the Nationals in Springfield, Missouri. When I found out that I was going to go on a plane to Springfield, Missouri, my heart skipped a beat. I was so excited! When the day finally came, I had to wake up at 4:00 a.m. because I had to be at the airport by 6:00 a.m.

As we were aboarding the plane, I was saying goodbye to my parents. They couldn't come because they had to go to work. Finaly, I got on the plane and sat next to my friends. I asked them what it was like being on a plane, and they said that it's fun. Then I calmed down a little.

The planes engine started and I was nervous again. As the plane started to move, I could see my parents watching from the window. I wanted to go back, but it was too late. The plane was going faster and I could hear the engine getting louder and louder until finaly we took off. The ground faded as we got higher. Then all I could see was the clouds.

It was a long ride there, but I got through it. On the way there, I played cards, checkers, and ate some food. My friends really helped me get through the ride. I even forgot about the landing! When it was time to land, the flaps on the wings of the plane went up and we started to go down. We were going fast and were almost at the ground. All of a sudden, there was a huge thump, and we were on the ground. The brakes were squeeky, but they worked. We were in Springfield!

We got off the plane and went to the hotel. It was nice. We got ready for the first game. The game was tough, but we won. The second game was that day also. We won it, too. The next day we won two more games. Then it was time for the last game, the championship. I scored the winning run. Everybody jumped on me, and that was fun.

What made it so special to me was that this was the first time in my life that I have been out of California. It was the first time I've ever won the Nationals, meaning we are the top team in the whole nation. We got the best award anybody could ever have. We even got to be on the news about 10 times! That, my friends, was the best thing that ever happened to me!

## Commentary

This paper demonstrates a good understanding of the task, addressing all parts of the writing prompt. However, the writer has some difficulty maintaining a steady focus. The title suggests that winning the championship is the focus of the paper. Yet the first paragraph and most of the paper focus on the writer's travel experience. The concluding paragraph incorporates both the travel and playing experiences.

The events of the narrative are sufficiently developed, although the details could be richer. Limited descriptions, a shortage of sensory detail, and an inconsistent focus are the main reasons this paper scores three points instead of four.

The writer presents main ideas and related details in separate paragraphs, demonstrating a firm grasp of organizational structure. The writer also uses a variety of sentence types, making the essay more interesting. There are some errors in grammar, punctuation, capitalization, and spelling, but these do not interfere with the reader's understanding.

*(Go on to the next page.)*

The following sample represents a narrative that meets the criteria for a 2-point paper.

### Christmas Day

The best thing that ever happened to me was on Christmas day! My whole family comes together and we talk about what has been going on in our lives. I just played with my cousins. They are nice to me most of the time because they are so much older than me. That day my cousin Jewel who is around my age, we both went to the movies with the older kids. We had to put up a fight for it not a real one. They think that we are too young to go places with them. We went anyways and it was a lot of fun.

It happened when I was about twelve years old. A few years younger compared to my older cousins. I still have a couple around my age.

This took place in my grandmother's house. Her house is like no other in the world! Some call it strange I do, maybe it is her own style, anyways the reson that I say that my grandmother's house is strange is because right when you walk into her house there is Elvis posters and little Elvis toys, and even an Elvis clock too. So do you think that she likes Elvis presely? Uh-huh!

It was so special to me because it is a time where everyone no matter where you are come together and realized what you have is specail. So don't take your family for granded. I know I won't.

**Commentary**

The paper's first sentence presents the topic of this paper. However, the writing task has been addressed only superficially, demonstrating the writer's limited understanding of the purpose for writing. The writer lacks a clear focus. For example, one significant event—attending the movies with older relatives—is described in a muddled way. The writer then abandons the main idea and moves on to a discussion of his or her grandmother's house. There are few details, and descriptive language is limited.

While there is an effort to develop paragraphs, the overall organization needs improvement. Sentence structure is often weak; however, the student does use a limited variety of sentence types. The paper has several errors in spelling and punctuation that may interfere with the reader's understanding.

The following sample represents a narrative that meets the criteria for a 1-point paper.

The best thing that ever happened to me was when I was eight years old. I had spent the night over at my best freind's house. He had just got a rily cool dog and we played with him all night.

When I got home the next day, I askd my mom what would she think about getting a dog. She said she would think about it so for one month I kept asking for the dog, then it was chrismas when I woke up there was a little puppy laying on top of me.

Me and my freind marcus would always talk about one of the dogs being better. The thing that made it so specail was that i had my own dog to brag about.

**Commentary**

This paper briefly outlines two special events in the writer's life—spending the night with a friend and receiving a puppy. It is unclear which of these events is intended as the focus for this paper. The writer offers no title and there is no topic sentence in the first paragraph to make the paper's focus clear to the reader. The student attempts to address the writing prompt but succeeds only at a superficial level. The lack of details and description are typical of a paper scoring one point. Evidently, the writer did not understand the purpose of the writing assignment.

While the sentences are arranged in a logical order, there is no variety in sentence type. The paper has serious errors in spelling, grammar, punctuation, and capitalization that interfere with the reader's understanding.

# Sample How-to Papers

Before you begin the evaluation process, you may want to examine the following student papers and commentaries. The papers are examples of student writing at each level of the rubric. The commentaries provide explanations of why each paper received its rating.

The following sample represents a how-to paper that meets the criteria for a 4-point paper.

---

### Jumping on a Scooter

Scooters are very mobile, and you can do lots of tricks with them. If you don't know what a scooter is, it is a piece of metal aluminum with wheels on each side. On top of the front wheel there is a post with handlebars to hold on to. In this paper, I will teach you the process of actually jumping with the scooter.

To jump with the scooter, you must have the following essential items:
- a scooter* with the proper grip tape (so you don't fall)
- foam handlebars
- polyurethane wheels
- hand gloves (optional)
- protective knee pads, elbow pads, and forearm pads
- helmet
- tennis shoes
- comfortable clothing

*It must be a quality brand scooter. Try not to get a cheap, cheap, cheap scooter.

The items listed above are very important. The other important thing is the type of surface you will be riding and jumping on. The surface should be smooth with no potholes. Potholes can really hurt your wheels if they get stuck. Also, make sure there are no major rocks in the area.

Before you can jump with your scooter, you must learn to glide. First, put your hands on the handlebars. Don't grip too tightly or too loosely. You must be relaxed. Second, put one foot in the middle of the scooter. Bend your knees and shift your weight to your toes and push off with your other leg. Then, put that foot on the scooter behind your first foot. It does not matter if you use your right or your left foot to push off. You should be gliding now. If not, you must practice a little bit more.

Once you have perfected gliding, you are now ready to jump. When doing all tricks the first time, always start slowly. The jump you are about to do is called the Bunny Hop. Start gliding, then bend your knees. Grip the handlebars, then jump so that your knees touch your chest. At the same time, pull up the handlebars. You have just done the Bunny Hop. Start practicing, and when you've mastered this, try jumping over small objects and speed humps!

---

## Commentary

This student has a clear understanding of the purpose for writing and has thoroughly addressed the writing prompt. The how-to paper starts with a good title and introduction, stating the skill to be learned and describing what a scooter is. The student immediately lists the materials needed to perform the jump, along with extra information that could be helpful to the reader.

This how-to paper has a clear, consistent organizational structure, including an engaging introduction and conclusion. The student presents the task clearly and in a logical order, stating the steps in the process and using sequence words and paragraphs to delineate ideas. The writer offers clear, concise directions that are easy to follow. In addition, the student demonstrates mastery of the conventions of English. The few errors that are present do not impede the reader's understanding of the paper. This paper is an excellent example of a skillfully written how-to paper at the seventh-grade level.

*(Go on to the next page.)*

The following sample represents a how-to paper that meets the criteria for a 3-point paper.

## Fix Your Hair

One thing I know how to do well is putting my hair up in small sections with the use of tiny rubberbands. This hairstyle is very popular with young girls in this day and age. It's fast, easy, and fun! After one lesson, you will be a pro.

Very few materials are needed in order to complete this. You need small rubberbands by Goody. These usually come in a bag full of 200. You can purchase this item almost anywhere hair products are sold. You also need one regular-sized hair tie. These are also provided by Goody. These come in a bag of 8. You can also buy this where hair styling items are sold. Extra-hold hair spray is good, preferably Pantine Pro-V. The last thing you need is a separating comb.

Before you start, make sure you wash your hair thoroughly. Do not try to do this hairstyle when your hair is dry. It will not turn as well as if it is wet and brushed out nicely and neatly.

To start the hairstyle, first use the separating comb to part your hair down the middle of your head. Step 2, using the separating comb, separate your hair from right behind your left ear, all the way to your right ear. Tie up the extra hair in the back with the regular size hair tie so it won't get in the way. Next, use the separating comb to divide the sections from the part in the middle of your head. The sections should be about 1-inch square. Make sure to divide a section one at a time, then spray a little hair spray and use 1 rubberband to tie it up. Continue until you get to your ear. Repeat on the other side of your head. To complete the hair style, spray hair spray onto your hair so the hair style will stay nice and neat for a whole day. Have fun with your hair!

## Commentary

This writer presents an organized how-to paper that addresses all aspects of the writing prompt. The writer maintains her focus, organizes main ideas into paragraphs, and provides supporting details. The introductory paragraph is engaging and appealing to the writer's intended audience. The writer gives specific details about the materials that are needed for the task, and steps are sequenced logically.

The variety of sentence types is one of this paper's strengths. Its greatest weakness is its fourth paragraph, in which the writer describes the steps of the process. More elaborate directions would be helpful to readers who have never attempted this hairstyle.

There are some errors in grammar, punctuation, capitalization, and spelling, but these do not interfere with the reader's understanding of the task.

*(Go on to the next page.)*

The following sample represents a how-to paper that meets the criteria for a 2-point paper.

## Playing Soccer

You probably have heard of the sport soccer, but have you ever actually played soccer? The sport soccer is not very popular in America, but in other parts of the world such as, Europe, Central and South America. In fact in many countries, soccer is called futbol (football). I'm going to teach you how to play soccer, what you need to play soccer, and how to practice.

If you watch an experienced soccer team playing, you should take to notice that there are players that run, run, run, and they don't get the ball. This is because they need to be in the position that they could help another player if need be. They also are not wearing the clothes they wear to school or work either. They are probably wearing a uniform or practice uniform, and long socks. To play soccer you should wear loose clothes so that you can run easily, preferably shorts and a tee shirt. Wearing these clothes is still not enough, you are also going to need soccer equipment for your safety. You are going to need soccer cleats, shin guards, and also long soccer socks to cover the shin guards. Soccer cleats are special shoes made for playing soccer, the cleats you get should fit comfortably and not be too loose and not too tight either. They also need to have no toe cleat or spike on the toe for the safety of you and your opponent, because the toe cleat could cause you to trip, or cause injury your opponent when you're trying to get the ball. Shin guards are a type of soccer equipment that protects your shins, because if you're playing then you can get accidentally kicked in the shins. The socks you get should be your size and fit comfortably. When you are putting on your socks remember to put them over the shin guards so the shin guards don't move while you are running or you can get hurt. Also when you by your equipment make sure that it is not too heavy and going to weigh you down. So when getting ready to practice you put on your uniform, shin guards, soccer socks, and then your soccer cleats.

Now that you know what to wear, you need is to your size soccer ball. The soccer balls com in sizes such as, size three for 4-8 year olds, size four for 8-12 year olds, and size five for 12 year olds and up. With eight and twelve year olds they need the ball to be the size for what age they are when they start the season. The ball also needs to be properly inflated. To see how inflated the ball is you put the ball against your chest and push lightly on the same square, and it should go in about 1/4th an inch it's properly inflated.

Now that you have all the equipment all you need is a soccer field to practice on and another person to help you with practicing. To practice you should start out with stretching such as flamingos, or keeping your legs straight and trying to touch the grass, and running some laps. Next try passing with each other and then kicking hard into an area (shooting), and other things such as dribbling, kicking/shooting. So, now you know most of the basics of soccer.

## Commentary

This paper demonstrates earnest effort, familiarity with the topic, and some understanding of the purpose for writing. The first paragraph promises the reader that the writer will discuss "…how to play soccer, what you need to play soccer, and how to practice." Had the subsequent paragraphs fulfilled the writer's promise, they should have followed a different sequence. However, that point is irrelevant given that the writer provides few details regarding how to practice for or play soccer.

The overall organization of the paper is adequate, although for the most part, the conclusion is absent. There are errors in the conventions of the English language that may make reading difficult.

*(Go on to the next page.)*

The following sample represents a how-to paper that meets the criteria for a 1-point paper.

## Computers

I am going to explain to you how to use a computer. I like playing games, going on the Internet and goint to programs, but a computer can do much more, but first before I tell you how to use a computer I will tell you what a computer is. A computer is a mechanic item that lets you go on the Internet, talk with people, go on the web, download stuff, go into programs, and can let you play games.

O.K. now I will tell you the steps you use for using a computer. First buy a computer. second hook up your computer in your house and then turn on your computer and start enstal programs, when you first turn on the computer the computer will gide you to programs, tells you how to use the keyboard and mouse, and lets you download program you want. Then when you are done download a Internet program so you can go on the Internet and start going on web sites, make your own email address and start downloading stuff. Well you can still do allot of stuff with out going on the Internet. For the busnes people you can make data tables, type, print, draw and listen to music. For kids you can record your voice, play games, paint write to your girlfriend, take picture of you doggies, and other kinds of stuff kids do.

There are much more to a computer than playing games so please buy a computer.

## Commentary

This student attempts to address the writing prompt; however, he or she chose an inappropriate topic for a how-to paper. While the student uses sequence words and orders the basic steps in the process, the topic is too complex for the student to explain adequately. Thus the reader is left unable to complete the steps and use a computer.

While the writer does give a sense of enthusiasm for the task, he or she has little understanding of the purpose of the writing assignment. The paper lacks a strong introduction and conclusion, directions are muddled, and sentence structures are weak. The paper has a number of serious errors in spelling, punctuation, and grammar that impede the reader's understanding.

# Sample Persuasive Papers

Before you begin the evaluation process, you may want to examine the following student papers and commentaries. The papers are examples of student writing at each level of the rubric. The commentaries provide explanations of why each paper received its rating.

The following sample represents a persuasive movie review that meets the criteria for a 4-point paper.

---

### Remember the Titans

A wonderful film to see is called <u>Remember the Titans</u>. It is a must-see film. I love the way the film mixes the topics of segregation and integration with football. It gives everyone who sees the film something to think about.

A coach from out of town moves to a southern community of blacks and whites. This new coach, Coach Boone, is a young black man who is there to try-out as the new coach for high school. He gets the job and the black boys in high school are extremely excited! Not everyone is excited, though, as you'll find out when Coach Boone has his first team meeting.

Coach Boone is determined to make sure that the team is fully integrated. When they went to Ghettysberg camp, Coach Boone made sure that no one of the same race would room together. He made the boys do three-a-day practices until all of the boys, black or white, got on the same social level. There is a scene where the boys are doing a practice and a young black boy and white boy start to associate. They show the rest of the team it's okay to be friends, even if your skin color is the opposite of mine. The next day the lunch hall was filled with laughter from both races. They were all talking, together.

When you see the movie, you'll find out about all the problems Coach Boone and the team faced, even though they all got along. This movie will touch your very soul, bring a smile to your lips, and a tear to your eye. This is why it is a must-see movie.

---

## Commentary

Clearly, this writer enjoyed seeing *Remember the Titans*. The writer tells us in the first paragraph that the movie's themes of segregation, integration, and football make this a movie worth seeing.

The writer addresses all parts of the writing task, showing a clear understanding of the purpose for writing. This is a well-developed review, in which the writer summarizes the film's highlights without disclosing too many details. The writer seems to have a sense of what information is important and what will appeal to his or her audience.

The organizational structure of the essay is well developed and logical, with strong opening and closing paragraphs. The writer employs a variety of sentence types to keep the review interesting and follows the conventions of English. Existing errors are few and do not interfere with comprehension.

*(Go on to the next page.)*

The following sample represents a persuasive movie review that meets the criteria for a 3-point paper.

## Pearl Harbor

The best movie I have seen recently is <u>Pearl Harbor</u>. I saw it on the 4th of July. It was a sad story about love, friendship, and family. The movie was so realistic, it was like I was really there.

<u>Pearl Harbor</u> is diffrent from other movies. It is nothing like I have seen before. I almost cried during the movie. Also, nobody has done a historic movie since <u>Titanic</u>. To me, <u>Pearl Harbor</u> was better and more tragic than <u>Titanic</u>.

Some movies are loved because they are funny, but I like this movie because it teaches everyone a lesson. It also lets us observe on what happened on that historic day. At the end of the movie, everyone in the movie is sad. The two main characters fall in love, and they remember their friends who had died in the war.

I think other people should see this movie so they can share my experiences. Although it was sad, <u>Pearl Harbor</u> was a good movie.

**Commentary**

This movie review addresses all parts of the writing task and shows a general understanding of purpose. It is adequately developed, with a mainly consistent point of view. While the student includes reasons for seeing the movie, he or she does not elaborate upon them. The absence of meaningful supporting details is this review's greatest weakness.

The student demonstrates an understanding of organizational structure and includes a variety of sentence types. There are some errors in grammar and spelling, but none that hampers understanding.

The following sample represents a persuasive movie review that meets the criteria for a 2-point paper.

## The Others

The best movie I have seen recently is The Others. The Others is the best movie to me because there is a twist ending and it is scarey through the whole movie.

What makes this movie different from others is it just scared me more than some of the other movies I have seen for a long time. I really liked this movie because of the ending.

I think others should see this movie because it is a scarey movie. Everybody who likes scarey movies should go see it because I really like the acting in the movie.

**Commentary**

The writer addresses some parts of the writing task but demonstrates little understanding of the purpose for writing. The first mention of the writer's desire for others to see this movie doesn't come until the last paragraph.

The writer fails to state the reasons that make the movie worth seeing in a clear and logical manner. Consequently, the reader must sift through the content to learn that the movie's surprise ending, frightening content, and acting are its positive features.

The review is minimally developed. It offers few details and little content to enable the reader to visualize the movie. There are also several errors in grammar, spelling, and punctuation that may interfere with a reader's understanding.

*(Go on to the next page.)*

The following sample represents a persuasive movie review that meets the criteria for a 1-point paper.

## The Outsiders

the outsidrs is a great movie. It's about this boy named Ponyboy who lost his mom and dad years ago now he lives with his brothers Sodapopand Darrie. Soon he stumbles into a hole lot of bad things with to Socs.becaues he and Jonny flirted with their X girl freinds Cherry and Marcia .After it all ends Pony boy gets a old letter from his dead freind Jonny befor he died it spoke of a poem that Ponyboy could not under stand it ment stay gold Stevie Wounder sang a song called stay gold for this classic movie and Emilio Estives and Tom Cruz were also in volved in this movie by playing roles like freinds of the main charter and S.E. Hinton the writer of this story was offered he part as a nures. All in all the outsiders a great movie even though it has violence and cussing please step outside and see this movie!!

## Commentary

This student addresses one part of the writing task—identifying a favorite movie. However, the student offers no reasons why someone might want to see the movie. The absence of persuasive reasons demonstrates that the writer had little or no understanding of the purpose for writing.

The review summarizes the movie's plot but lacks a persuasive focus. The writer fails to establish main ideas and organize them in any sensible way. Errors in grammar, spelling, and punctuation overwhelm this paper, making it difficult for the reader to understand. This writer needs considerable guidance if he or she is to write a truly persuasive movie review.

# Proofreading Marks

Use the following symbols to help make proofreading faster.

| Mark | Meaning | Example |
|---|---|---|
| (oval) | spell correctly | I liek dogs. |
| ⊙ | add period | They are my favorite kind of pet. |
| ? | add question mark | Are you lucky enough to have a dog? |
| ≡ | capitalize | My dog's name is scooter. |
| ℐ | take out | He is a great companion for me and my my family. |
| ∧ | add | We got Scooter when *he* was eight weeks old. |
| / | make lower case | My Uncle came over to take a look at him. |
| ∽ | trade places | He watched the puppy run in around circles. |
| ⋏ | add comma | "Jack that dog is a real scooter!" he told me. |
| ⌄ ⌄ | add quotation marks | Scooter! That's the perfect name! I said. |
| ¶ | indent paragraph | ¶ Scooter is my best friend in the whole world. He is not only happy and loving but also the smartest dog in the world. Every morning at six o'clock, he jumps on my bed and wakes me with a bark. Then he brings me my toothbrush. |

# The Writing Process

In writing, you can use a plan to help you think of ideas and then write about them. This plan is called a *writing process*. Here are the steps of the writing process.

## Step 1: Prewriting

Think about why you are writing. What is your purpose, or goal? Who are you writing for?

Choose a topic, or something to write about. Make notes. Organize your notes in a way that makes sense.

## Step 2: Drafting

Use your ideas and notes from the first step to begin writing.

## Step 3: Revising

Read your draft. Is the purpose of your paper clear?

Share your writing with someone else. Talk about what is good about your paper and what could make it better.

## Step 4: Proofreading

Correct any mistakes you find in spelling, grammar, punctuation, and capitalization.

## Step 5: Publishing

Make a clean copy of your paper.

Share your paper with others.

## Moving Back and Forth

All together, there are five steps in the writing process. However, as you write, you may move back and forth through the steps several times before you reach your writing goal.

You may return to your draft many times to make it better. Go back and forth often. The extra steps will improve your writing and help you publish your best work.

Name _____     Date _____

# Types of Writing

In this book you will read examples of different kinds of writing. Then you will practice your own writing skills. You will write to...

- **Tell a Story**

  A story is also called a narrative. A narrative has...
  - one or more characters.
  - a setting, or place and time for the story to happen.
  - a plot that includes a problem that is solved step by step.

- **Tell About a Part of Your Life**

  An autobiographical sketch tells about part of your life. It includes...
  - important events that happened to you.
  - details that describe the events that happened.

- **Describe Someone or Something**

  When you describe something or someone, you share details. Details can be...
  - facts.
  - information that comes from using your senses of hearing, sight, smell, touch, and taste.
  - dialogue, or words that people say.
  - thoughts and feelings.

- **Explain How to Do Something**

  When you explain how to do something, you talk about...
  - the materials someone needs.
  - the steps someone should follow in order.
  - important details.

- **Show How Two Things, Places, or People Are Alike and Different**

  To explain how two things are alike and different, you...
  - use reference materials to find information on a topic.
  - organize main ideas about the topic to show how two things
    are alike.
  - organize main ideas about the topic to show how two things
    are different.
  - include important details.

# Types of Writing, page 2

- **Share Information in a Short Report**

  To write a good report, you…
  - choose a specific topic.
  - decide what you would like to learn about your topic.
  - use reference materials to collect information about your topic.
  - use facts, not opinions.

- **Convince Someone**

  When you write persuasively, you…
  - share your opinion or position on a topic.
  - try to make someone agree with you.
  - try to convince someone to do something.

# A Model Paper

## A Personal Narrative

### Locker Laws

Sometimes it's hard being an older sister, especially when you have a brother like mine. He's so cheerful all the time. Plus, he's excited about starting middle school next year. It's only February, and he's still in fifth grade, but he's already excited. I've tried to tell him there's not so much to be excited about, but so far I haven't convinced him. The first lesson I tried to teach him was about lockers. You see, of all the reasons there are to go to middle school, my brother thinks having a locker is the best reason of all.

I have tried to explain that there are some middle-school laws that aren't written in any school handbook. They're not posted in the hallway or on the bulletin board in the office. They just exist. Only middle-school students know what they are. They're a secret to everyone else. So, I tried to explain the laws about lockers.

First, I told him he'd better start practicing deep-knee bends. I described the lockers at our school. Two rows of lockers line every hallway. One of the laws every middle-school kid knows is that the tall kids get the lockers on the bottom. If you're tall, and my brother is, then you ought to practice deep-knee bends every morning before you get to school. That will be the only thing that keeps you in shape. Plus, you'll have to learn how to bend with one arm up in the air. I explained that you use the arm to protect your head. That's because the rule that makes tall kids get the bottom lockers is the same rule that gives short kids the top lockers. While you're on your knees, I told him, they're on their toes. At least once a day, the kid on top loses his or her balance. The kid's books fall with the kid, and there, I say with a short demonstration, is where your arm comes in handy.

He watched carefully and seemed to understand. I thought I had convinced him that his first locker wasn't going to be the highlight of middle school, but I was wrong. He smiled and started doing deep-knee bends. My brother is amazing.

So I tried to give him another lesson in locker reality. We talked about the locks. I explained that a lock never works when you're in a hurry. It will work any other time, but not when you're in a hurry. That means if you don't remember to get your track shoes out before you slam the door shut, you're going to be late for gym. The coach isn't going to listen to any excuses, and you and all the other kids who couldn't get their lockers open will run extra laps. You can blame the second law of lockers. Every middle-school kid knows that a lock only has one good spin a day. After that, you have to beg, scream, and fight to get it open. You also have to be ready to take the consequences when you're late for class.

I stopped to look at my brother again. His face looked serious, so I thought I was getting through. Then, he started stretching like you do before you run laps. He really is amazing.

Okay, fine, laws one and two didn't make much difference, so I moved to the third law. That's the law of egg salad sandwiches. This law, I explained, says that if even one kid in the whole school eats egg salad for lunch, that kid has the locker above yours. Your nose finds your locker before you do. The smell attaches itself to everything in your locker, including your gym clothes. People won't make fun of you, of course. They know you didn't get to pick your locker. However, you can't expect them to eat lunch with you.

I looked closely at my brother. His eyebrows met in the middle. He seemed to be thinking hard. Then he ran into the bathroom. When he came out, he had a can of air freshener in his hands. "This should take care of law number three," he said. I shook my head. I don't think I'm going to win this battle.

I had only one locker law left—the surprise clean-out. I explained that at least once in every grading period, your homeroom teacher makes the whole class clean out their lockers. You never know when these days are coming, and if you aren't prepared, the word *embarrassed* is not enough to describe how you feel. Middle-school teachers know just the right time for a clean-out. It's always the day that you forget to take home your dirty gym shorts. It's the day when your overdue library books are bursting to get out. It's the day a colony of fruit flies escapes from the science lab and finds the rotting apple in your locker. It's the day when the Valentine card you got for the girl who sits next to you in homeroom falls out and lands at the girl's feet.

I thought for sure that mentioning the Valentine card would do the trick. My brother gets bashful around girls. I waited for him to say something. He disappeared again, this time into his bedroom. When he came out, he handed me a card. I opened the card and read it aloud. It said, "To My Sister on Valentine's Day." My brother smiled and gave me a hug. Now I was embarrassed. What an amazing kid! He's going to love middle school.

# Respond to the Model Paper

**Directions** > Write your answers to the following questions or directions.

1. What are the first and second locker laws?

   The first law was tall people get bottom lockers and short people get top lockers and the second was the lockers do not open when you are in a hurry, and you will be late to class

2. What are the third and fourth locker laws?

   The third law is don't eat egg salad because it will stink up your locker and the forth is make sure your locker is clean or a suprise locker clean out will come and you may be inbarresed

3. Write a paragraph to summarize the story. Use these questions to help you write your summary:

   • What are the four locker laws?
   • How does the brother respond to each locker law?
   • How does the story end?

   The nurrarator stated there are four locker laws, The first law is that tall people get bottom lockers and short people get top lockers, her brother didnt care. The second law was not to be late to gym because of your locker because you will have to run another lap, and still her brother didnt care. The third locker law is dont bring egg salad for lunch because you locker will stink. He brother just got up and got air freshener. The forth and last locker law is make sure you clean out your locker alot orelse your teacher may have a locker clean out and a valintines card from a girl in home room will fall out in front of her and you will be inbarrased Her brother just left the room. In the end her brother came out of his room with a valintines card to her.

# Analyze the Model Paper

 **Directions** → Read "Locker Laws" again. As you read, think about how the writer wrote the story. Write your answers to the following questions.

1. How do you know that this is a personal narrative?

   I know this is a person narrative because the girl is telling her story.

2. Read the first paragraph again. What problem does the writer present in this paragraph?

   The problem was the brother was excited to go to middle school and the sister thought he was crazy.

3. The writer interrupts her explanations of the locker laws with descriptions of her brother's reactions. Why do you think she does this?

   She does that because she wants us to know how he feels because her brother is super excited about middle school

4. In the fourth and sixth paragraphs, the writer describes her brother as amazing. She says it again in the last paragraph, but this time, she adds an exclamation point. What do you think the writer is trying to tell you?

   because her bother was stretching and bending and geting ready for middle school.

# Writing Assignment

 **Directions** ➤ Think about someone you know who is special to you. Write a personal narrative about this person. Use examples and details to show why this person is special. Use this writing plan to help you write.

## Writing Plan ════════════════════════════

**Who is the person you will write about?**

**Tell what makes this person special to you.**

**Give examples to show why this person is special.**

# First Draft

---

## Tips for Writing a Personal Narrative:

- Write from your point of view. Use the words *I* and *my* to show your readers that this is your story.

- Think about what you want to tell your reader.

- Organize your ideas into a beginning, middle, and end.

- Write an interesting introduction that "grabs" your readers.

- Write an ending for your story. Write it from your point of view.

## First Draft

**Directions** ⟩ Use your writing plan as a guide for writing your first draft of a *Personal Narrative*.

_____

_____

_____

_____

_____

_____

_____

_____

_____

_____

_____

*(Continue on your own paper.)*

# Revise the Draft

**Directions** ➤ Use the chart below to help you revise your draft. Check *Yes* or *No* to answer each question in the chart. If you answer *No*, make notes to remind yourself how you can revise, or change, your writing to improve it.

| Question | Yes ✔ | No ✔ | If the answer is no, what will you do to improve your writing? |
|---|---|---|---|
| Does your story describe someone special to you? | | | |
| Do you introduce the special person in the first paragraph? | | | |
| Do you use specific examples to explain why this person is special? | | | |
| Do you describe events in the order they happened? | | | |
| Do you include important details? | | | |
| Does your conclusion summarize your story in a new way? | | | |
| Do you tell your story from your point of view? | | | |
| Have you corrected mistakes in spelling, grammar, and punctuation? | | | |

**Directions** ➤ Use the notes in your chart and writing plan to revise your draft.

# Writing Report Card

**Directions** ⟩ Read your revised draft again or ask someone else to read it. Have the person who reads your paper complete the following Report Card. Revise your paper until you have no less than a Very Good Score for each item.

Title of paper: _____

Purpose of paper: _____ This paper is a personal narrative. It talks about someone who is special to me.

Person who scores the paper: _____

| Score | Writing Goals |
|---|---|
| | Is the story told from a first-person point of view? |
| | Does the story have a strong beginning, or introduction? |
| | Does the story include specific examples to explain why the person in the story is special? |
| | Are there details to support each example? |
| | Do events in the story happen in order? |
| | Are there different kinds of sentences, such as questions, dialogue, and descriptions, that help make the story interesting? |
| | Does the story have a strong ending, or conclusion? |
| | Does the writer make it clear why the person described in this narrative is special? |
| | Are the story's grammar, spelling, and punctuation correct? |

☺ Excellent Score     ☆ Very Good Score     + Good Score

✔ Acceptable Score     — Needs Improvement

# A Model Paper

## An Autobiographical Sketch

### *No Ordinary Experience*

I remember listening quietly as my parents talked about our new home. It was no surprise to any of us that we were moving again, but no one had expected this to happen. The Air Force was sending us to Okinawa. No one in my family had a clue where Okinawa was until I found the atlas. Together, we searched among the tiny islands of the Pacific Ocean until we found it. There it was, at the end of a chain of islands below Japan.

Finding the island on the map didn't make me feel any better about moving. Our family had already moved three times and I was barely thirteen. I knew I would miss Charlie, my neighbor and best friend. Three years would feel like forever. Charlie and I would be sixteen years old before we saw each other again.

I should have known that these three years would be unusual. My first clue was the summer we spent in California. There weren't enough houses on Okinawa for families, and we had to wait our turn. Two weeks before my dad left, my parents drove us to an air base in California where we moved into an apartment. Lots of other families were living there, too. There were loads of kids my age. I think half of them belonged to the same family. I loved the Mercer kids. We spent mornings at the base pool and afternoons at the movies, where we could get in for fifty cents. Sometimes our moms drove us all to our favorite park where we'd have picnics and spend the day playing ball. Even though I missed Charlie, this summer was moving up on my list of favorite summers.

My second clue that this experience would be different from the others came on the airplane. We had left California and were excited to be on our way to Honolulu, Hawaii. We had to stop there first because the plane couldn't hold enough fuel to get us all the way to Okinawa. I had never been to Hawaii before. I didn't care that we wouldn't be allowed to leave the airport. I was glad to be there and eager to see something. Inside the airport, my mother bought two necklaces of flowers, one for me and one for my little brother. She explained that in Hawaii, people give these necklaces as gifts. Mine was beautiful. It was made from dozens of small white flowers. I had never had anything like it. I took it off before we got back on the plane. I didn't want to crush the petals. I put the necklace on my lap, which turned out to be a mistake. Hours later, the plane's humming had put me to sleep. However, my brother was wide-awake and looking for something to do. When I opened my eyes again, my necklace was still on my lap. But it didn't have any flowers on it. My brother had picked every petal, leaving me a string. You can imagine what I wanted to do to him.

Eventually, we reached the island. We were going to live on a hill outside the gates of the air base until a house on base became available. We were excited until we saw the hill and the house.

Tall bamboo grass grew up the sides of the hill and alongside the hill's only road. Halfway up, part of the hill had been cut away. That's where our house was. Our house was one of three houses that could fit on the hill. The rest of the space was covered with tombs. We were living next to a cemetery!

At first, I thought my dad couldn't have found a creepier place for us to live, but once I got used to them, I didn't notice the tombs at all. Then on special holidays, women dressed in beautiful robes came to pray. Sometimes the women left gifts of food outside the tombs. My brother and I knew these days were special, so we stayed indoors, occasionally peeking from a window. The seriousness of the occasion made the people beautiful to watch.

On school days, the bus waited for my brother and me at the bottom of the hill. Then in the afternoon, the bus dropped us off in the same place. Twice each day we walked down and up the hill alongside bamboo that was three times taller than we were. My brother kept his eyes on one side of the road, while I watched the other side. We walked slowly, looking out for the dangerous snakes that we had been told lived in the bamboo forests. Luckily, we never saw one.

In the storm season, when we had warnings of typhoons, my brother and I helped cover the windows in our house with boards. We also helped fill the bathtub, jars, and pots and pans with water. We never knew how long we would have to live without clean water and electricity.

We also never knew what was living in our house with us. We checked closets for snakes and looked inside our shoes before we put them on. Roaches longer than my thumb lived everywhere, even inside the washing machine. It took months for us to find out how they got in our refrigerator. I remember a time when my mom opened the fridge and saw a huge roach walking across her fresh lemon pie. That was the last straw, or I should say, roach. Mom slammed the door shut and went straight to the base to ask for a new refrigerator. It came the next day. The movers took the old refrigerator away and then called later to tell us what they found. An entire roach colony was living in the space between the walls of the refrigerator.

Our family had lots of friends on the island, but just like in California, we found one special family that we visited often. Tony was my age. His sister Sylvia was sixteen. When we were with Sylvia, we listened to music and practiced the latest dances. When Tony, my brother, and I were on our own, we searched through the caves behind Tony's house. Late one Sunday afternoon, as we were saying goodbye, the ground began to shake. We froze and watched our car rock back and forth. The car wasn't the only thing rocking. That was my first and only earthquake experience.

I'm lucky. Lots of people take expensive vacations to have the kinds of adventures we had on Okinawa. How many other people get to learn about holidays for the dead, typhoons, poisonous snakes, roaches, and earthquakes without leaving home?

# Respond to the Model Paper

**Directions** ➤ Write your answers to the following questions or directions.

1. In an autobiographical sketch, a writer talks about something important that happened to him or her. What important thing happened to this writer?

_____

_____

_____

2. How would you describe the setting for this story?

_____

_____

_____

3. What is the first clue the writer gives you to explain why this was no ordinary experience?

_____

_____

_____

4. Write a paragraph to summarize the story. Use these questions to help you write your summary:

   • What are the main ideas in this story?
   • What happens first? Second? Third?
   • How does the story end?

_____

_____

_____

_____

_____

_____

# Analyze the Model Paper

**Directions** ▷ Read "No Ordinary Experience" again. As you read, think about how the writer wrote the story. Answer the following questions.

1. This story has an optimistic mood, or feeling. How did the writer create this mood?

   _____
   _____
   _____

2. Read the fourth paragraph again. What does the writer do to bring *you* into the experience?

   _____
   _____
   _____

3. What does the writer use in the tenth paragraph to keep the story's mood positive?

   _____
   _____
   _____

4. How does the writer use the last paragraph to convince you that this was no ordinary experience?

   _____
   _____
   _____
   _____
   _____
   _____
   _____
   _____

# Writing Assignment

 **Directions** Write an autobiographical sketch about something important that happened to you. Write about something you remember well. Use this writing plan to help you write.

## Writing Plan

> **What important thing happened to you?**
>
>
>
>
>

> **What happened first? How will you describe it?**
>
>
>
>
>

> **What happened second? How will you describe it?**
>
>
>
>
>

> **What happened last? How will you describe it?**
>
>
>
>
>

# First Draft

---

## Tips for Writing an Autobiographical Sketch:

- Write about something important that happened to you.
- Write about something you remember well.
- Give details that help explain your experience.
- Describe events in the order that they happened.

## First Draft

**Directions** Use your writing plan as a guide for writing your first draft of an *Autobiographical Sketch.*

_____

_____

_____

_____

_____

_____

_____

_____

_____

_____

_____

_____

_____

*(Continue on your own paper.)*

# Revise the Draft

**Directions** ▷ Use the chart below to help you revise your draft. Check *Yes* or *No* to answer each question in the chart. If you answer *No*, make notes to remind yourself how you can revise, or change, your writing to improve it.

| Question | Yes ✔ | No ✔ | If the answer is no, what will you do to improve your writing? |
|---|---|---|---|
| Does your autobiographical sketch describe something important that happened to you? | | | |
| Does your story have a clear setting? | | | |
| Do you include important characters in your story? | | | |
| Do you describe events in the order they happen? | | | |
| Do you use specific details to help tell your story? | | | |
| Have you corrected mistakes in spelling, grammar, and punctuation? | | | |

**Directions** ▷ Use the notes in your chart and writing plan to revise your draft.

Name _____  Date _____

# Writing Report Card

**Directions** ➤ Read your revised draft again or ask someone else to read it. Have the person who reads your paper complete the following Report Card. Revise your paper until you have no less than a Very Good Score for each item.

Title of paper: _____

Purpose of paper: ___ This paper is an autobiographical sketch. It describes something important that happened in my life. ___

Person who scores the paper: _____

| Score | Writing Goals |
|-------|---------------|
|  | Is this story an example of an autobiographical sketch? |
|  | Is the setting described in detail? |
|  | Does the writer use important characters to help tell the story? |
|  | Does the writer describe specific events? |
|  | Does the writer use important details to help explain events? |
|  | Does the writer describe events in the order they happen? |
|  | Does the writer convince you that this experience was important to him or her? |
|  | Are the story's grammar, spelling, and punctuation correct? |

☺ Excellent Score   ☆ Very Good Score   + Good Score

✔ Acceptable Score   — Needs Improvement

# A Model Paper

## A Descriptive Story

### *Jambalaya Weekend*

For Les and Wes Bateaux, finding something interesting to do on the weekends wasn't hard. After all, they were easy to please. There were three things they loved most. The first was their dog, Poe. The second was being outside. The third was food, any kind of food. When you live in Cajun country, the last two are easy to find. And Poe, well, Poe is easy to find, too. Look for the Bateaux brothers and you'll find Poe either ahead or behind, chasing the scent of food.

Two weekends ago, the brothers and Poe went to a swamp festival near their home. Poe sat with them in their pirogue, or canoe, as they paddled through water filled with alligators. Ashore, the brothers took turns tossing popcorn shrimp to Poe. Poe made the brothers proud. He had, after all, learned to catch popcorn shrimp before he was even six months old. Now he never missed. A series of quick jaw snaps could take a pound of popcorn shrimp out of the air in minutes.

Last weekend, the brothers took Poe to a fair. Wes and Poe ate sour, mouth-pinching pickle chips while they watched Les lose at the ring toss. Les had never been very good at ring tosses, so Wes tried. It didn't take long before Wes won a life-sized stuffed alligator. What better way to celebrate such a victory than with the beignets they loved so much? Each bite into these fried pillows of dough sent clouds of powdered sugar into the air.

This weekend the brothers were in the mood for another fair. It was already Friday, and they didn't have any plans. Wes was starting to think they might have to stay at home when he heard Les drive up to the house.

Poe came in first. Then came Les. Both of them looked like soaked muskrats. "Whew," Les said as he took off his rain hat and hung it on a hook by the door. Poe shook hard, sending arrows of water in every direction. "Look, Wes!" said Les, pointing to a flyer he held in his hand. "I found one! The Frog Festival is tomorrow. Do you remember how close we came to winning the frog-racing contest last year? Let's try again this year. What do you say?"

"I don't know," said Wes. "If it's raining like this tomorrow, we may have to hop like frogs just to get there. Heck. Let's go anyway. We'd better visit the creek to find a new frog."

"Yee-hah!" Les yelled, as he slapped his leg. "Come on, Poe. Let's go. There's nothing like a rain to bring out the frogs." Les grabbed his hat and a fishing bucket off the porch as he and Poe headed to the creek. "Come on, Wes, it's getting dark. If we're going to find a winner, we need to start now."

Saturday arrived, and the two brothers and Poe jumped into their truck. The sky didn't own a single cloud, and the air smelled of magnolia flowers and barbecue. The brothers were excited when they saw how many people had shown up for the fair. At the ticket counter, Les bought the tickets while Wes asked where to sign up for the frog-racing contest. "If it's the frog-racing you want, you'd better hurry," said the lady selling tickets. "The contest is about to start. You'll need to sign in and get a number for your frog. The frog-jumping contest comes later. You have plenty of time before you have to sign up for that one."

"We want the first one," Les said. "We've got a winner, I know it."

On their way to the racing grounds, the brothers and Poe passed booth after booth of spicy treats. Red pepper and other spices tickled their noses. Blackened catfish sizzled on grills. Curls of pink shrimp floated in giant soup pots. The brothers' eyes widened to take it all in. There were shelves lined with orange sweet-potato pies. There were bowls as big as kitchen sinks filled with steaming black-eyed peas, tomatoes, and okra. Tables held stacks of fried crab cakes bigger than dessert plates. There was no end to the food. The brothers were frozen with delight until Poe barked sharply. The brothers jumped like nervous frogs at the noise.

"We almost forgot why we're here," Wes said. "Say no more, Poe. We're on our way."

If the brothers had ever made it to the frog-racing grounds, this story would be longer. But the jambalaya got in their way. Before reaching the grounds, the brothers passed a huge black pot sitting over an open fire. The cook stood on a ladder, stirring the thick stew with a canoe paddle. The brothers stopped to sniff. That ended their frog's chances of winning the racing contest. The smells of sweet rice, shrimp, crab, and oysters held the brothers captive. Even Poe seemed to have lost all interest in the race.

"You know, Wes, surely by now that race has started, don't you think? There's no point in going over there now."

"I think you're right, Les. Poe, let's stop here awhile and give our new green friend a chance to stretch his legs. He needs to warm up before the jumping contest this afternoon. Speaking of warming up, I'm ready for some jambalaya. What about you?"

"I'm ready," Wes said with excitement. "I don't think weekends ever get better than this, do you?" he asked. The brothers watched Poe wag his tail and lick his lips. "See," said Wes, "even Poe agrees."

# Respond to the Model Paper

**Directions** Write your answers to the following questions or directions.

1.  Describe the setting where the brothers live.

    _____

    _____

2.  How does the writer let you know that the brothers love food?

    _____

    _____

3.  Why didn't the brothers make it to the frog-racing contest?

    _____

    _____

4.  Write a paragraph to summarize the story. Use these questions to help you write your summary:

    • What are the main ideas of the story?
    • What happens first? Second? Third?
    • How does the story end?

    _____

    _____

    _____

    _____

    _____

    _____

    _____

    _____

    _____

    _____

    _____

# Analyze the Model Paper

 **Directions** ⟩ Read "Jambalaya Weekend" again. As you read, think about how the writer achieved his or her purpose for writing. Write your answers to the following questions or directions.

1. Read the fifth paragraph again. Name one simile and one metaphor the writer uses in this paragraph.

   _____

   _____

   _____

2. The writer uses some unusual words in this story, such as *Cajun, pirogue, beignet,* and *jambalaya.* Why are these words important to the story?

   _____

   _____

   _____

3. Draw a picture of the description in paragraph 12.

4. Write a paragraph to describe what you think the brothers and Poe did the weekend after the Frog Festival.

   _____

   _____

   _____

   _____

   _____

   _____

   _____

# Writing Assignment

To describe something, a writer uses interesting words to tell what he or she sees, hears, feels, tastes, and smells. The writer also compares things to other things, like a wet dog to a soaked muskrat. Describe something that you and a relative or friend did together. Use this writing plan to help you write.

## Writing Plan

 What experience would you like to describe? Write it in the circle. Then write words, similes, or metaphors that describe the experience on the lines.

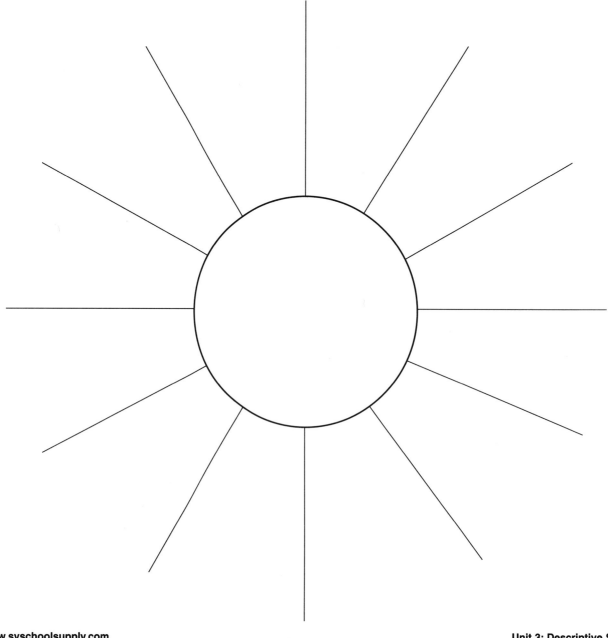

# First Draft

---

> ## Tips for Writing a Descriptive Story:
> - Use your voice when you write. That means you should use your special way of expressing yourself.
> - Help readers see, smell, taste, feel, and hear what you are writing about.
> - Use interesting words to help you describe.
> - Use similes and metaphors to help your readers imagine the experience you are writing about.

## First Draft

**Directions** ➤ Use your writing plan as a guide as you write your first draft of a *Descriptive Story*.

_____

_____

_____

_____

_____

_____

_____

_____

_____

_____

_____

*(Continue on your own paper.)*

Name _____   Date _____

# Revise the Draft

**Directions** ▷ Use the chart below to help you revise your draft. Check *Yes* or *No* to answer each question in the chart. If you answer *No*, make notes to remind yourself how you can revise, or change, your writing to improve it.

| Question | Yes ✔ | No ✔ | If the answer is no, what will you do to improve your writing? |
|---|---|---|---|
| Do you focus on something that happened to you and a relative or friend? | | | |
| Do you describe what you see, hear, smell, taste, and feel? | | | |
| Do you use action words to describe what happens? | | | |
| Do you use descriptive similes and metaphors? | | | |
| Do you describe events in the order they happen? | | | |
| Have you corrected mistakes in spelling, grammar, and punctuation? | | | |

**Directions** ▷ Use the notes in your chart and writing plan to revise your draft.

# Writing Report Card

 **Directions** ➤ Read your revised draft again or ask someone else to read it. Have the person who reads your paper complete the following Report Card. Revise your paper until you have no less than a Very Good Score for each item.

Title of paper: _____

Purpose of paper: _____ *This paper is a descriptive story. It describes* _____

_____ *something a friend or relative and I did together.* _____

Person who scores the paper: _____

| Score | Writing Goals |
|---|---|
| | Does this story describe an experience that happened to the writer and a friend or relative? |
| | Does the writer describe what he or she sees, hears, tastes, smells, and feels? |
| | Does the writer use interesting action words? |
| | Does the story include descriptive similes and metaphors? |
| | Are the events that happen in the story in order? |
| | Are the story's grammar, spelling, and punctuation correct? |

☺ Excellent Score      ☆ Very Good Score      + Good Score

✔ Acceptable Score      — Needs Improvement

# A Model Paper

## A How-to Paper

---

### *Make Your Own Snowstorm*

Have you ever wished you could make snow at any time of the year? Ski resorts often use snow machines to add more snow to their slopes, even in the summer. Now you, too, can make your own snow. All you need is a simple cold chamber that you assemble yourself.

There are a few materials you'll need to do this project. They include:

- a large can or pail
- a second can that fits inside the large can
- a towel
- dry ice*
- a foam cooler to hold the dry ice
- tongs to handle the dry ice
- a nail or small file to shave the dry ice
- thick gloves
- a flashlight
- regular ice
- salt
- safety goggles

*Be careful when you handle the dry ice!  It causes severe freezing burns if your skin touches it. Ask an adult to help you.

Now you're ready to build a cold chamber. First, put on your safety goggles. Then add regular ice and salt to the large can and mix them together. Next, put the small can on top of the ice. There should be enough ice in the large can to make the mouth of the small can even with the mouth of the large can. In the space between the cans, pack more of the ice and salt mixture. To protect your hands, wear gloves while packing the ice. Also, wrap a towel around the large can, as this container will become very cold.

In a short time, the space inside the small can will also become very cold. You can test this by breathing into the can. You should see a small cloud form.

Next, to make snow, you'll need to seed your cloud. This process is like the process farmers use when they seed clouds for rain. Farmers seed clouds with tiny grains of dust or silver that attract water droplets. The water droplets come together to form raindrops. At ski resorts where people use snow machines to make snow, the seeds are particles of a natural protein that attracts water droplets.

Snow normally forms in a cloud only if temperatures are very cold. However, bits of dry ice can work as seeds in clouds that are too warm to make snow the usual way. Dry ice is carbon dioxide in its solid form. When dry ice is dropped into clouds that are too warm to form snow, water droplets in the clouds freeze into crystals. Eventually, these crystals become snowflakes. You will use bits of dry ice as seeds in your cold chamber.

Ask an adult to use the tongs to hold the dry ice. Then, wearing gloves and being careful not to let your skin touch the dry ice, use a nail or small file to shave tiny pieces into your cloud. As you do so, ask the adult to shine a flashlight into the small can. You should see several tiny ice crystals begin to form. Breathe gently into the cloud again to add moisture. Then wait two minutes before breathing into the cloud again. In time, your breaths will produce enough moisture for the ice crystals to grow bigger. Eventually, they will become heavy enough to fall out of the cloud as snowflakes.

Now that you understand how snowflakes form, you can make your own snow any time. All you need are a helper, a few materials, and time. You might want to try this project again in July when the sun is blazing and you're ready to cool off.

# Respond to the Model Paper

**Directions** ⟩ Write your answers to the following questions or directions.

1.  Why do you have to be careful not to let dry ice touch your skin?

    _____

    _____

2.  How do farmers seed clouds?

    _____

    _____

3.  Why do you breathe into the cloud chamber?

    _____

    _____

4.  Draw a picture of a cloud chamber like the one the writer describes. Label the different parts of the chamber.

# Analyze the Model Paper

 **Directions** ⟩ Read "Make Your Own Snowstorm" again. As you read, think about why the writer wrote this paper. What did the writer do to help explain how to make a snowstorm? Write your answers to the following questions or directions.

1.  Name at least two things that make this paper a good example of a how-to paper.

   _____

   _____

2.  Why does the writer include the warning about working with dry ice?

   _____

   _____

3.  Why does the writer list the materials you need to make a snowstorm before telling you how to do it?

   _____

   _____

4.  Why does the writer use words like *first, next,* and *then*?

   _____

   _____

5.  What is the purpose of the last paragraph?

   _____

   _____

   _____

   _____

   _____

   _____

Name _____     Date _____

# Writing Assignment

 **Directions** ➤ Think about something you want to tell others how to do. Use this writing plan to help you write.

## Writing Plan

**What will you tell others how to do?**

**List the materials someone will need.**

**Write the steps someone should follow in order. Number the steps.**

**Write some sequence words that help the reader know what to do.**

# First Draft

### Tips for Writing a How-to Paper:

● Choose one thing to teach someone.

● Focus on a plan.

    1. Think of all the materials someone will need.

    2. Think of all the steps someone will follow.

● Use sequence words in your directions.

## First Draft

**Directions** ⟩ Use your writing plan as a guide as you write your first draft of a *How-to Paper*.

_____

_____

_____

_____

_____

_____

_____

_____

_____

_____

_____

_____

*(Continue on your own paper.)*

# Revise the Draft

Use the chart below to help you revise your draft. Check *Yes* or *No* to answer each question in the chart. If you answer *No*, make notes to remind yourself how you can revise, or change, your writing to improve it.

| Question | Yes ✔ | No ✔ | If the answer is no, what will you do to improve your writing? |
|---|---|---|---|
| Does your paper teach someone how to do something? | | | |
| Do you introduce the project or task in the first paragraph? | | | |
| Do you include safety warnings if they are necessary? | | | |
| Do you include all of the materials someone needs? | | | |
| Do you explain all of the steps someone must follow? | | | |
| Are the steps in order? | | | |
| Do you explain each step clearly so that it is easy to follow? | | | |
| Do you use sequence words to help guide your reader? | | | |
| Have you corrected mistakes in spelling, grammar, and punctuation? | | | |

**Directions** Use the notes in your chart and writing plan to revise your draft.

# Writing Report Card

**Directions** ⟩ Read your revised draft again or ask someone else to read it. Have the person who reads your paper complete the following Report Card. Revise your paper until you have no less than a Very Good Score for each item.

Title of paper: _____

Purpose of paper: ___ **This paper explains how to do something.** ___

Person who scores the paper: _____

| Score | Writing Goals |
|---|---|
| | Does the writer introduce the topic in the first paragraph? |
| | Does the paper teach someone how to do something? |
| | Does the paper include necessary safety warnings? |
| | Does the paper include the materials someone needs? |
| | Does the paper explain each step someone will follow? |
| | Are the steps in order? |
| | Is each step written clearly to make it easy to follow? |
| | Are there sequence words to help the reader understand? |
| | Are the paper's grammar, spelling, and punctuation correct? |

☺ Excellent Score     ☆ Very Good Score     + Good Score

✔ Acceptable Score     − Needs Improvement

# A Model Paper

## A Compare and Contrast Paper

### *Precious Spices: Salt, Pepper, and Saffron*

Though you might find it hard to believe, people have worked and fought for spices. Among the most valued spices are salt, pepper, and saffron. You may shower your French fries with salt or sprinkle extra pepper on your hamburger. You may enjoy the color and smell of saffron rice. Chances are, you don't give these spices a second thought. Nevertheless, throughout history people have made and spent fortunes for these spices.

Let's look at ordinary table salt first. Salt is found in seawater, in salt wells, and beneath the ground. Heat energy is needed to remove salt from seawater. Large pools of water are left in the sun. Also, large pans of salt water may be placed over fires. Water evaporates and leaves salt behind.

A salt well is like an oil well. Two pipes, one inside the other, are drilled into the ground. Fresh water is pumped down. Salt in the soil dissolves in the water. As more fresh water is forced down, the salt water is forced up. Once it's on the surface, the water is treated like ocean water. That is, it's heated until it evaporates and leaves the salt behind.

Salt is also part of rocks almost everywhere around the world. People dig mines beneath the ground and use machines to break the rock salt apart and bring it to the surface. It is crushed to different sizes and bagged or boxed for consumers. In our hands or on our food, salt is a grainy, white substance with no scent.

Salt has a long history. Even in ancient times, people used salt for different purposes, including seasoning and preserving their food. Almost 5,000 years ago, Chinese people wrote about salt in their books of medicine. In ancient Egypt salt was used to preserve dead bodies. In ancient Rome soldiers were paid in salt. Some say the word *soldier* comes from the words *sal dare*, which mean to give salt. Salt was once pressed into coins more valuable than gold. Thus, people have fought wars and traveled far to find and control it.

Pepper is another important spice. Unlike salt, pepper begins as a berry. Pepper plants are shrubs that climb like vines or trail across the ground. They grow where it is hot, such as in Indonesia. Pepper plants form small green berries about the size of a pea. As the berries ripen, they turn red. When they change color, the berries are picked, cleaned, and dried. Whether they bake in the sun or over fires, as they heat, the berries turn black. The berries are then ground to make a powder. The powder may be black, white, or red, depending on the kind of pepper plant that made the berries and the process used to make the pepper. No matter the color, pepper has a scent and sharp taste that make it easy to identify.

In the early days of trade between Europe and India, pepper was so expensive that it was reserved for royalty. A king or queen might receive a few pounds of pepper as a gift. One king named Alaric I is said to have demanded pepper to stop his attack on Rome in 408 A.D. Hippocrates, the father of medicine, thought pepper helped the heart and kidneys work. Even today, people use pepper as a medicine.

Saffron comes from the female parts of the purple saffron crocus, a flower. Each flower must be picked by hand in the autumn when the flowers are fully open. It may take up to 250,000 flowers to make one pound of saffron. That helps explain why saffron is one of the most expensive spices you can buy. Saffron is sold in the form of a yellow-orange powder or as slender red threads. Most of the world's saffron crocus flowers are grown in India, Iran, and Spain.

Like salt and pepper, saffron is used to season food and as medicine. In India, hosts give their guests food flavored with saffron as a sign of honor. People also use saffron to treat or prevent diseases, such as the common cold.

Records show that people in ancient Egypt and Rome used saffron as a dye. They also used it to make perfumes and medicines and to season food. Traders carried the spice through Asia, and in time, through Europe. Because the spice was expensive, people used it as a sign of their wealth and power. The ladies in the court of King Henry VIII, for example, used saffron to dye their hair.

Pay attention to the spices on your table or in your food the next time you visit your favorite restaurant. Salt, pepper, and saffron may seem like ordinary spices. In fact, you might not be willing to spend your allowance to buy them. However, they are anything but ordinary, and people have paid far more to have them. Salt, pepper, and saffron are some of the world's precious spices.

# Respond to the Model Paper

**Directions** ➤ Write your answers to the following questions or directions.

1.  Why are salt, pepper, and saffron called *precious* spices?

    _____

2.  What are some spices you use?

    _____

3.  Summarize the story by making a chart. Use the chart below to list ways salt, pepper, and saffron are alike and different.

## A Compare and Contrast Chart
## for
## Salt, Pepper, and Saffron

| How Salt, Pepper, and Saffron Are Alike | How Salt, Pepper, and Saffron Are Different |
|---|---|
|  |  |

# Analyze the Model Paper

 **Directions** ▷ Read "Precious Spices: Salt, Pepper, and Saffron" again. As you read, think about how the writer achieved his or her purpose for writing. Write your answers to the following questions or directions.

1. Identify three important main ideas the writer uses to describe each spice.

_____

_____

_____

_____

_____

2. Why do you think the writer uses the same main ideas to describe each spice?

_____

_____

_____

_____

_____

3. Identify one important detail about each spice that supports the title of this paper.

_____

_____

_____

_____

_____

4. How are the first and last paragraphs related?

_____

_____

_____

_____

Name _____  Date _____

# Writing Assignment

 **Directions** ⟩ People around the world have favorite foods. Learn about foods in two countries, such as India and China. Write about how the foods in those countries are alike and how they are different. Use this writing plan to help you write.

## Writing Plan

Choose two countries you want to write about. Call them A and B.

A = _____          B = _____

Use what you know, books, or the Internet to learn more about the food in countries A and B. Learn about three main ideas: which foods people eat most, which spices they use, and how they prepare the foods. For each main idea, list what is true only about A in the A circle. List what is true only about B in the B circle. List what is true about both A and B where the two circles overlap.

**Main Idea:**
Foods people
eat most

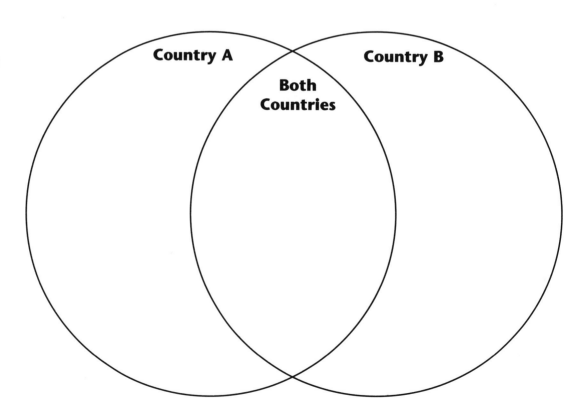

# Writing Assignment, page 2

**Main Idea:**
Spices people
use most

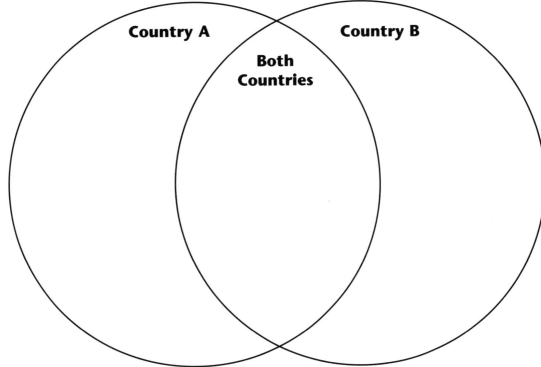

**Main Idea:**
How the foods
are prepared

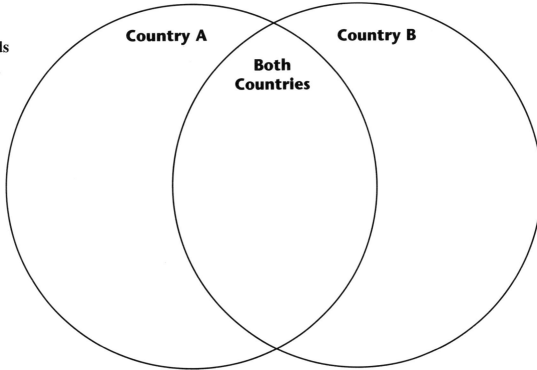

# First Draft

Tips for Writing a Compare and Contrast Paper:

- Find information about foods in your countries.
- Organize the information you find into main ideas.
- Use details to explain each main idea.
- Explain how the foods are alike.
- Explain how the foods are different.
- Use your last paragraph to summarize your main ideas in a new way.

## First Draft

**Directions** ▸ Use your writing plan as a guide as you write your first draft of a *Compare and Contrast Paper*.

_____

_____

_____

_____

_____

_____

_____

_____

_____

_____

_____

_____

*(Continue on your own paper.)*

# Revise the Draft

**Directions** ▸ Use the chart below to help you revise your draft. Check *Yes* or *No* to answer each question in the chart. If you answer *No*, make notes to remind yourself how you can revise, or change, your writing to improve it.

| Question | Yes ✔ | No ✔ | If the answer is no, what will you do to improve your writing? |
|---|---|---|---|
| Do you introduce the subjects you will write about in the first paragraph? | | | |
| Do you explain how the foods in two countries are alike? | | | |
| Do you explain how the foods in two countries are different? | | | |
| Do you have more than one main idea about the foods in each country? | | | |
| Did you organize the main ideas into paragraphs? | | | |
| Do you use details to support each main idea? | | | |
| Do you summarize the main ideas of your paper in your conclusion? | | | |
| Have you corrected mistakes in spelling, grammar, and punctuation? | | | |

**Directions** ▸ Use the notes in your chart and writing plan to revise your draft.

Name _____  Date _____

# Writing Report Card

**Directions** ▸ Read your revised draft again or ask someone else to read it. Have the person who reads your paper complete the following Report Card. Revise your paper until you have no less than a Very Good Score for each item.

Title of paper: _____

Purpose of paper:  This paper shows how foods in two countries are alike and different.

Person who scores the paper: _____

| Score | Writing Goals |
|---|---|
| | Does the writer tell what the paper will be about in the first paragraph? |
| | Does the paper explain how the foods in two countries are alike? |
| | Does the paper explain how the foods in two countries are different? |
| | Does the writer use more than one main idea to describe the foods in both countries? |
| | Does the writer include details to support each main idea? |
| | Does the writer organize the paragraphs in a way that makes sense? |
| | Does the last paragraph summarize what the paper is about? |
| | Are the paper's grammar, spelling, and punctuation correct? |

☺ Excellent Score    ☆ Very Good Score    + Good Score

✔ Acceptable Score    − Needs Improvement

# A Model Paper

## A Short Report

### *Clues from the Past*

Once a plant or animal dies, it begins to decay, or break down. That's how a body ends up as a skeleton. This process happens naturally unless nature or people interfere. Then the dead body is preserved.

A preserved body is a body that is treated so that it does not break down. Unlike a skeleton, a preserved body keeps some of the soft materials it had while the person was alive. These materials include skin, muscles, and organs. In nature, bacteria and fungi help break down a body. They need oxygen and water to do their work. In some places, oxygen is missing. Bogs, or land that is soft and wet, are an example. In other places, water is frozen. Glaciers are an example. If oxygen is missing or if water is frozen, bodies don't break down. They can look as they did when the people died. That's why even today, people find bodies in bogs.

Bogs can preserve bodies so well that bodies thousands of years old can have skin, eyes, and hair. Scientists study the bodies they find in bogs to learn how people lived. Bodies may have food in their intestines that tell scientists what these people ate. They may wear clothing that gives information, such as what the weather was like where these people lived. Bodies also tell secrets. They tell scientists why people died. Scientists look for signs of disease, accidents, and crime. There may also be objects buried nearby, such as jewelry and weapons. These objects tell scientists even more about people who lived long ago.

Ice preserves bodies, too. In 1991, hikers found a body while hiking in the Alps. Near the body, police and scientists found several tools, including an axe, a bow and arrows, and a small knife. The body wore a cape made from grass. It also wore a bearskin cap and leather shoes lined with grass. Scientists who studied the body determined that "Ötzi, the Ice Man" had lived about 5,000 years ago. He probably herded animals in the mountains.

People also prevent bodies from decaying. People in ancient Egypt, for example, believed that after death, a person moved to another world. They also believed the person needed the physical body that was left behind. Thus, it was important to keep the body in good condition. So the Egyptians embalmed the body, or treated it with chemicals to preserve it. These preserved bodies are called mummies.

While the Ice Man was herding animals in the Alps, Egyptians were preserving their dead. The process, called mummification, took about 70 days. First, the embalmer, a special priest, removed all of the body's organs except the heart. Egyptians believed the heart was the center of a person's being. They also thought a person's intelligence lived in the heart. The organs removed from the body were preserved, too, and placed in special boxes and jars. Later in Egyptian history, embalmers would embalm the organs and then put them back into the body.

The body then had to be dried. Priests covered the body with natron, a natural salt. They also put packets of natron inside the body. When the body was dry, the packets were removed and the body was rinsed. By this time, the body was shrunken and very dry, but still obviously human. Sometimes strips of cloth called linen were used to fill in spaces on the body. The body might also be given false eyes.

The next step in making a mummy was adding the linen cloth. Priests wrapped the body with yards and yards of linen. Sometimes each finger and toe was wrapped separately before it was wrapped again as part of a hand or foot. Between layers of cloth, the priests coated the body with warm resin that gave the finished mummy a hard, smooth finish.

The mummification process was expensive. Few common people could afford it. Thus, it was members of the royal family who were mummified most. Using today's technology, scientists can learn much about Egyptian history by studying mummies. X-rays, for example, let scientists see inside the mummy without removing the wrappings. They can study small bits of bone to learn how tall people were and how long they lived. They can study unwrapped skin, fingernails, and hair to learn about the diseases Egyptians suffered and the medicines they took. And DNA samples let scientists make connections among branches of royal family trees.

The Egyptians aren't the only people to preserve their dead. Mummies have been found around the world, including in Asia, South America, North America, and Greenland. People in ancient Peru, for example, salted their dead. They wrapped their mummies in reed mats and then buried them under the floors of their houses. In Papua, New Guinea, the dead were smoke-cured and covered in clay. Then they were propped up so that they overlooked their villages. One of the most well-preserved mummies was found in China. The mummy, an embalmed woman who was an important person in the Han Dynasty, still has her skin, hair, fingernails, and even eyeballs.

Mummies teach us many things. They teach us about daily life and beliefs among people who lived thousands of years before us. They teach us about disease and medicine. They also teach us about the processes of preserving the dead. Whether created through natural or human means, preserved bodies are a link to the past.

# Respond to the Model Paper

**Directions** ▶ Write your answers to the following questions or directions.

1.  Why do bogs prevent decay after death?

    _____

    _____

    _____

2.  Why do glaciers prevent decay after death?

    _____

    _____

    _____

3.  Why is the Ice Man unusual?

    _____

    _____

    _____

4.  Write a paragraph to summarize the report. Use these questions to help you write your summary:

    • What are the main ideas in this report?
    • How did the Egyptians make mummies?
    • Why are scientists interested in mummies?

    _____

    _____

    _____

    _____

    _____

    _____

    _____

    _____

# Analyze the Model Paper

 **Directions** ➤ Read "Clues from the Past" again. As you read, think about the main ideas the writer tells about. Write your answers to the following questions.

1.  In the first paragraph, the writer says that decay happens unless nature or people interfere. Paragraphs 2–4 talk about the ways nature interferes. What do the paragraphs beginning with paragraph 5 talk about?

    _____

    _____

    _____

2.  Read the sixth paragraph again. Why do you think the writer mentions the Ice Man in this paragraph?

    _____

    _____

    _____

3.  Read the tenth paragraph again. Why do you think the writer included this paragraph?

    _____

    _____

    _____

    _____

4.  How is the first paragraph related to the last paragraph?

    _____

    _____

    _____

    _____

    _____

    _____

    _____

# Writing Assignment

In a short report, writers write about one topic. They find information about the topic. Then they use the information to choose the main ideas for their report. They also choose details to help explain each main idea.

 **Directions** ▷ Write a short report about a science topic that interests you. Your idea might even come from the report "Clues from the Past." Use this writing plan to help you write.

## Writing Plan

The topic of this paper is:

_____

Main Idea of Paragraph 1: _____

Detail: _____

Detail: _____

Detail: _____

Main Idea of Paragraph 2: _____

Detail: _____

Detail: _____

Detail: _____

Main Idea of Paragraph 3: _____

Detail: _____

Detail: _____

Detail: _____

# First Draft

## Tips for Writing a Short Report:

- Find information about your topic.
- Take notes about main ideas important to your topic.
- Take notes about important details for each main idea.
- Organize the main ideas and details into paragraphs.
- Put paragraphs in a logical order.
- Use the last paragraph to summarize your report.

## First Draft

**Directions** → Use your writing plan as a guide as you write your first draft of a *Short Report*.

_____

_____

_____

_____

_____

_____

_____

_____

_____

_____

_____

_____

_____

*(Continue on your own paper.)*

# Revise the Draft

**Directions** ➤ Use the chart below to help you revise your draft. Check *Yes* or *No* to answer each question in the chart. If you answer *No*, make notes to remind yourself how you can revise, or change, your writing to improve it.

| Question | Yes ✔ | No ✔ | If the answer is no, what will you do to improve your writing? |
|---|---|---|---|
| Does your report focus on one topic? | | | |
| Do you introduce your topic in the first paragraph? | | | |
| Do you have more than one main idea to explain your topic? | | | |
| Do you organize your main ideas into paragraphs? | | | |
| Do you include details to explain each main idea? | | | |
| Do you use your last paragraph to summarize your report? | | | |
| Have you corrected mistakes in spelling, grammar, and punctuation? | | | |

**Directions** ➤ Use the notes in your chart and writing plan to revise your draft.

Name _____     Date _____

# Writing Report Card

**Directions** ▷ Read your revised draft again or ask someone else to read it. Have the person who reads your paper complete the following Report Card. Revise your paper until you have no less than a Very Good Score for each item.

Title of paper: _____

Purpose of paper: _____ This paper is a short report. _____

Person who scores the paper: _____

| Score | Writing Goals |
|---|---|
| | Does this short report focus on one topic? |
| | Does the writer introduce the topic of this paper in the first paragraph? |
| | Does the writer use more than one main idea to explain the topic? |
| | Are main ideas organized into paragraphs? |
| | Are there details to explain each main idea? |
| | Does the report "stick" to the topic? |
| | Does the last paragraph summarize the report? |
| | Are the report's grammar, spelling, and punctuation correct? |

☺ Excellent Score      ☆ Very Good Score      + Good Score

✔ Acceptable Score      − Needs Improvement

# A Model Paper

## A Persuasive Letter

121 Earhart Lane
Los Angeles, California 90035

November 12, 2002

Station Manager
Space Age Channel Television Studio
P.O. Box 122
Washington, D.C. 20003

Dear Station Manager:

I am a big fan of your station. I think your educational programs about air and space are great. From one show, I learned that the first person to fly faster than the speed of sound was Chuck Yaeger. In another show, I learned that Neil Armstrong and Buzz Aldrin were the first people to walk on the moon. Now I watch your channel to learn about the International Space Station because I want to work there one day. Your channel has taught me a lot about the history of air and space travel. Even so, one important subject is missing. That subject is women. I've never seen a single program that describes the accomplishments of women in air and space.

Women have played important roles in powered flight since the early 1900s. Let me give you just a few examples. Bessica Raiche helped build the airplane she flew in 1910. Her first flight lasted only a few minutes, but she tried several more flights. Some call Raiche the "First Woman Aviator in America." In 1911, Harriet Quimby became the first American woman to earn a pilot's license. She was also the first woman to fly across the English Channel. In 1913, Katherine Stinson and her mother started a flying business. Two years later, Marjorie Stinson joined the company. She started a flight school to train WWI pilots from the U.S. and Canada.  In 1921, Bessie Coleman became the first African-American person to earn a pilot's license. She earned her license in France and then came back to the U.S. to raise money to build a flight school for other African-Americans.

I've given you only a few examples of the women who were part of America's air history. There are more. And the number grows even larger every year. By 1958, when NASA was formed, women were part of that, too. In fact, NASA's very first Chief Astronomer was Dr. Nancy Roman. Margaret W. Brennecke was a welder. She chose the metals and techniques for building the Saturn rockets that flew in the 1960s. She did the same for Spacelab and the Space Shuttle's rocket boosters. Many other women worked with the space program as engineers and scientists. In 1978, six women, including Dr. Sally Ride, joined NASA as astronauts. Twenty years later, Lt. Col. Eileen Collins became NASA's first female commander.

I've left out so many women. And so have you. Unless you include women, you're telling only half of the history of air and space travel.

Besides telling only half a story, you're missing the chance to send an important message to young girls and boys in school. Those children will probably grow up to live in space! This is a good time to tell all of them about how they can be a part of the future.

If you don't think preparing children for the future is your job, then you might think about the people who watch and support your channel now. My research tells me that more than half of the people who watch your channel are female. How long do you think they'll watch if you don't tell stories that include them? What will happen to your station when half of your viewers stop watching?

In closing, I'm asking you to include women in your station's programming. Tell women's stories to give a more complete history of air and space travel. Tell women's stories to help prepare young girls and boys for their future. Finally, tell women's stories to keep your viewers and your station! Act now so that I can watch your channel tomorrow.

Sincerely yours,

*Jen Rumi-Stevens*

Jen Rumi-Stevens
Future Space Station Commander

# Respond to the Model Paper

**Directions** ➤ Write your answers to the following questions or directions.

1.  Why is Jen writing to the station manager?

    _____

    _____

    _____

2.  List three reasons Jen gives to explain why the station manager should include more shows about women.

    _____

    _____

    _____

3.  Why do you think Jen mentions the number of women who watch the Space Age Channel?

    _____

    _____

    _____

4.  Write a paragraph to summarize the main points Jen makes in her letter. Use these questions to help you write your summary:

    • Why is Jen writing?
    • What reasons for adding shows about women does Jen give to the station manager?

    _____

    _____

    _____

    _____

    _____

    _____

    _____

    _____

# Analyze the Model Paper

 **Directions** Read the persuasive letter from Jen again. As you read, think about why she wrote this letter. Write your answers to the following questions or directions.

1.  Read the first paragraph again. Write the sentence that tells you what this letter is about.

    _____

    _____

    _____

2.  Read the second and third paragraphs again. Why do you think Jen includes this information?

    _____

    _____

    _____

    _____

3.  How do you think the station manager will feel after reading this letter? Why?

    _____

    _____

    _____

    _____

4.  Under her name, Jen calls herself a Future Space Station Commander. Why do you think Jen added this title?

    _____

    _____

    _____

    _____

# Writing Assignment

**Directions** In a persuasive letter, a writer tries to convince someone or a group of people to do something. The writer tries to make the reader feel a certain emotion about the topic he or she writes about. Write a persuasive letter to a friend to convince him or her to spend a weekend with you. Use this writing plan to help you write.

## Writing Plan

**1.** Write your address.

**2.** Write the date.

**3.** Write your friend's name and address.

**4.** Write a polite greeting, or salutation.

**5.** What will you say in the first paragraph to let your friend know why you are writing?

**6.** Complete the chart.

| Main Points You Will Present | Supporting Details You Will Use |
|---|---|
|  |  |

**7.** Use your last paragraph to write a conclusion. Summarize the important points you made.

**8.** Choose a friendly closing.

**9.** Sign your name.

# First Draft

---

## Tips for Writing a Persuasive Letter:

- Use a strong beginning to grab your reader's attention.
- Make your purpose for writing clear to the reader.
- Give reasons that will appeal to your reader's emotions.
- Organize your reasons from least important to most important.
- Use a strong ending that leaves your reader convinced you are right.

## First Draft ════════════════════════════

**Directions** ▷ Use your writing plan as a guide for writing your first draft of a *Persuasive Letter.*

_____

_____

_____

_____

_____

_____

_____

_____

_____

_____

_____

_____

_____

*(Continue on your own paper.)*

# Revise the Draft

**Directions** ▷ Use the chart below to help you revise your draft. Check *Yes* or *No* to answer each question in the chart. If you answer *No*, make notes to remind yourself how you can revise, or change, your writing to improve it.

| Question | Yes ✔ | No ✔ | If the answer is no, what will you do to improve your writing? |
|---|---|---|---|
| Is the purpose of this letter clear? | | | |
| Does the first paragraph grab your reader's attention? | | | |
| Do you give specific reasons to convince your reader? | | | |
| Are the reasons you use in order from the least to the most important? | | | |
| Do you appeal to your reader's emotions? | | | |
| Do you use the last paragraph to restate your opinion in a convincing way? | | | |
| Have you corrected mistakes in spelling, grammar, and punctuation? | | | |

**Directions** ▷ Use the notes in your chart and writing plan to revise your draft.

Name _____   Date _____

# Writing Report Card

 **Directions** Read your revised draft again or ask someone else to read it. Have the person who reads your paper complete the following Report Card. Revise your paper until you have no less than a Very Good Score for each item.

Title of paper: _____

Purpose of paper: _____ **This is a persuasive letter.** _____

Person who scores the paper: _____

| Score | Writing Goals |
|-------|---------------|
| | Is the writer's purpose for writing clear? |
| | Does the writer grab the reader's attention in the first paragraph? |
| | Does the writer give specific reasons to convince the reader? |
| | Are reasons presented in order from the least to the most important? |
| | Does the writer appeal to the reader's emotions? |
| | Does the last paragraph leave the reader convinced the writer is right? |
| | Are the letter's grammar, spelling, and punctuation correct? |

☺ Excellent Score      ☆ Very Good Score      + Good Score

✔ Acceptable Score      − Needs Improvement

# A Model Paper

## A Persuasive Movie Review

### *To Kill a Mockingbird*

Most of the time, I'm disappointed when I see a movie based on one of my favorite books. But *To Kill a Mockingbird* didn't disappoint me at all. In fact, I think everyone should see it. After they read the book, that is.

Made in 1962, the movie is in black and white, but don't let that stop you from seeing it. In some ways, the black and white colors help tell the story. For example, the colors create the movie's setting. The story happens in the early 1930s during the Great Depression. Times were hard for many people. There weren't enough jobs and many people were poor. You could say that the movie's plain colors help tell the story of *To Kill a Mockingbird* without words.

The black and white colors also stand for the struggle between people. For example, the story shows how different life was for black and white people living in the South in the 1930s. It also shows the struggle between prejudice and tolerance.

The Finch family lives in a small town in Alabama. Atticus Finch is a lawyer. A black man is accused of a crime he didn't commit. He's too poor to hire a lawyer, so the judge in the case assigns one. Ordinarily, that might not be difficult, but because the accused man is black as well as poor, the judge must choose carefully. He asks Atticus. Atticus believes in justice and takes the case because it's the right thing to do. However, some people who live in his town don't agree. They threaten him and his children, Jem and Scout.

Scout is six years old. She is the movie's narrator, that is, she tells the story. Jem is her older brother. When the story begins, school is out. Scout and Jem meet Dill, a boy Scout's age who's visiting his aunt for part of the summer. Together, the children look for interesting ways to fill hot and lazy summer days.

The children spend time in their treehouse telling stories. One of those stories is about a run-down house nearby and the people who live there. Here is an example of another struggle. This time it's a struggle between truth and lies. The children learn that what they believe about Mr. Radley, the man who owns the house, and his son, Boo, isn't true. At first, Boo is a frightening mystery. Then something awful happens and the children learn that Boo is their friend.

The children believe that Boo is crazy and that his father keeps him locked away. Consequently, the children are afraid to go near the house. One day, Scout, who is rolling inside a rubber tire, accidentally goes into the Radley's yard. The tire hits the front steps and Scout is too dizzy and too frightened to move. Jem rushes in to save her. Later, when Scout really does need help, it won't be Jem who protects her. It will be Boo.

It is Atticus's work that brings Boo outside to help Scout. While the children are solving the mystery of who is hiding small gifts in a tree, their father is defending his client, Tom Robinson. Feelings in the town are strong and set against Atticus and Tom. But Atticus doesn't back down, and matters get worse. Someone attacks Scout, and Boo must kill someone to save her.

This movie is one of the best movies ever made. First, it was based on an award-winning book by Harper Lee. She won the Pulitzer Prize for her book in 1961. Then, the movie was nominated for several Academy Awards in 1962, including Best Picture. But it's not the awards alone that make this movie worth seeing. Watch this movie because it tells a timeless story. It's a story that shows the opposites that exist in the world. It shows love and hate and truth and lies. It shows fear and bravery and right from wrong. Finally, it helps us see ourselves as the people we are and the people we can be. See *To Kill a Mockingbird* and I think you'll agree.

# Respond to the Model Paper

**Directions** ➤ Write your answers to the following questions or directions.

1. Who are the important characters in this movie?

   _____

   _____

   _____

2. Name two struggles the writer describes.

   _____

   _____

   _____

3. Identify the opposites that exist in the story.

   _____

   _____

   _____

4. Write a paragraph to summarize this movie review. Use these questions to help you write your summary:

   • What is the purpose of this paper?
   • What reasons does the writer give for seeing the movie?

   _____

   _____

   _____

   _____

   _____

   _____

   _____

   _____

# Analyze the Model Paper

 **Directions** ▷ Read the review of *To Kill a Mockingbird* again. As you read, think about the main ideas the writer gives to convince readers to see this movie. Write your answers to the following questions.

1. Why do you think the writer warns you that the movie is in black and white?

   _____

   _____

   _____

2. Why do you think the writer focuses mainly on the children in this review instead of Atticus and Tom?

   _____

   _____

   _____

3. Why do you think the writer mentions the awards the book and movie received?

   _____

   _____

   _____

4. What do the first and last paragraphs have in common?

   _____

   _____

   _____

   _____

   _____

   _____

Name _____     Date _____

# Writing Assignment

 **Directions** ▷ In a persuasive movie review, writers try to convince readers to watch a movie. What's your favorite movie? Write a persuasive movie review to convince your friends to see this movie. Use this writing plan to help you write.

## Writing Plan

**What is the name of the movie you will review?**

_____

Write reasons your friends should see this movie. Write details to support each reason.

**Reason #1**

_____

_____

**Details to support Reason #1**

_____

_____

_____

_____

**Reason #2**

_____

_____

**Details to support Reason #2**

_____

_____

_____

_____

**Reason #3**

_____

_____

**Details to support Reason #3**

_____

_____

_____

_____

**Reason #4**

_____

_____

**Details to support Reason #4**

_____

_____

_____

_____

# First Draft

Tips for Writing a Persuasive Movie Review:

- Make sure you have a strong opinion.
- Give good reasons to support your opinion.
- Give important details that support each reason.
- Grab your reader's attention in the first paragraph.
- Restate your opinion in the last paragraph.

## First Draft

**Directions** ⟩ Use your writing plan as a guide for writing your first draft of a *Persuasive Movie Review.*

_____

_____

_____

_____

_____

_____

_____

_____

_____

_____

_____

_____

*(Continue on your own paper.)*

# Revise the Draft

**Directions** ➤ Use the chart below to help you revise your draft. Check *Yes* or *No* to answer each question in the chart. If you answer *No*, make notes to remind yourself how you can revise, or change, your writing to improve it.

| Question | Yes ✔ | No ✔ | If the answer is no, what will you do to improve your writing? |
|---|---|---|---|
| Do you use your first paragraph to grab the reader's attention? | | | |
| Do you make it clear that you have a strong opinion? | | | |
| Do you give good reasons to support your opinion? | | | |
| Do you include details that help support each reason? | | | |
| Do you restate your opinion in the last paragraph? | | | |
| Does this review make your reader want to see this movie? | | | |
| Have you corrected mistakes in spelling, grammar, and punctuation? | | | |

**Directions** ➤ Use the notes in your chart and writing plan to revise your draft.

Name _____   Date _____

# Writing Report Card

**Directions** ▷ Read your revised draft again or ask someone else to read it. Have the person who reads your paper complete the following Report Card. Revise your paper until you have no less than a Very Good Score for each item.

Title of paper: _____

Purpose of paper: _____ This paper is a persuasive movie review. _____

Person who scores the paper: _____

| Score | Writing Goals |
|---|---|
| | Does the first paragraph grab the reader's attention? |
| | Is the writer's opinion clearly stated? |
| | Does the writer give good reasons for his or her opinion? |
| | Are there details to support each reason? |
| | Does the writer restate his or her opinion in the last paragraph? |
| | Does this review make you want to see this movie? |
| | Are the review's grammar, spelling, and punctuation correct? |

☺ Excellent Score   ☆ Very Good Score   + Good Score

✔ Acceptable Score   − Needs Improvement

Name _____     Date _____

# A Model Paper

## A Persuasive Essay

### *Take a Speech Class!*

What happened the last time you stood up to speak to your class? Did your knees shake so hard that your teacher went to the door to see who was knocking? Did your voice wobble so much that you sounded like a child's toy? Did sweat roll from under your arms down your sides and plop to the floor? Did your eyes blink so often you thought someone had turned off the lights? If your answer to any of these questions is yes, then you should take a speech class.

There are so many good reasons for taking a speech class that it's hard to decide where to begin. But I'll try anyway. Taking a speech class makes you confident. What does it mean to be confident? For one thing, it means you can stand up to talk without shaking like the last leaf on a tree in a heavy windstorm. It means you can speak in a language that sounds like English. It also means your classmates won't roll their eyes while you're talking. They'll be listening. And they'll listen because you sound like you know what you're talking about.

So, how do you make this happen? In a speech class, you'll learn to think before you speak. No doubt, you've heard that one before. But in this case, it's good advice. Here's why. You can't talk about something you don't know anything about. Well, I guess you could, but there go your classmates' eyes again. People can tell when the person who's talking to them doesn't know what he or she is talking about. They can also tell when someone isn't prepared to speak. You've probably noticed that yourself. How long does a speaker like that keep your attention? Not long.

Thinking before speaking can make you confident. This is what you will practice in a speech class. Let's say, for example, that on the first day of school, your teacher gives you a homework assignment. You must come to school the next day ready to tell the class how you spent your summer vacation.

The night before class, you could decide to "wing it." Basically, that means you don't think about the assignment at all. You think the most important thing you can do to prepare is to show up for class. Well, we know what happens when you do that. But if you can't remember, read the first paragraph again. Now, let's try again.

This time, sit down and take out some paper. Make a list of everything you did over the summer. If the list says only summer school, you have a problem. Your speech could be a disaster unless you add a little spice. I don't mean lie. I mean think harder! What happened in summer school? Whom did you meet? What special projects did you do? Whom did you sit with at lunchtime? Name two things you did that were outstanding. Do you understand where I'm going here?

Okay. Now that your list covers both sides of your paper, you're ready. Go through the list and choose one or two things you really want to talk about. Then get out a new piece of paper.

Don't write every detail. Go for the main ideas. List them in the order you want to talk about them. Then use a few words or phrases that will help you remember what you want to say about each main idea. When you reach the end, move to a mirror. That's right. Move to a mirror. Look yourself straight in the eye and start talking! Say everything you want to say to the class, and say it over and over again. Say it so often that you can remember what you want to say without using the piece of paper in your hands. You're almost ready.

The big moment comes. It's your turn to talk. You've practiced your speech. You know what you want to say. The problem is that the people out there don't look like the person in the mirror. But they are. They're just like you, only less prepared. Breathe deeply. Look at the crowd. Be brave. Move forward. This probably won't be the best speech you'll ever give, but it's a start. And after you finish your speech class, no one will ever hear your knees knock again.

# Respond to the Model Paper

**Directions** ➤ Write your answers to the following questions or directions.

1. Why should everyone take a speech class?

   _____

   _____

   _____

2. According to the writer, what does the word *confident* mean?

   _____

   _____

   _____

3. What's the first thing you learn to do in a speech class?

   _____

   _____

   _____

4. Write a paragraph to summarize the essay. Use these questions to help you write your summary:

   • Why should you take a speech class?
   • What are the main points the writer makes in this essay?

   _____

   _____

   _____

   _____

   _____

   _____

   _____

   _____

# Analyze the Writer's Model

**Directions** ▷ Read "Take a Speech Class!" again. As you read, think about the main ideas the writer discusses. Write your answers to the following questions.

1. What is the writer trying to do in the first paragraph?

   _____

   _____

   _____

2. Why do you think the writer uses humor to convince you to take a speech class?

   _____

   _____

   _____

3. Read the fifth paragraph again. Why do you think the writer directs your attention to the first paragraph again?

   _____

   _____

   _____

4. How are the first and last paragraphs related?

   _____

   _____

   _____

   _____

   _____

   _____

   _____

   _____

# Writing Assignment

Before a writer begins to write a persuasive essay, he or she forms an opinion. This opinion becomes the writer's purpose for writing. Then the writer gives specific reasons why the reader should have the same opinion.

 **Directions** ➤ Write a persuasive essay about a topic that is important to you. State your opinion clearly. Also offer important reasons for this opinion. Use this writing plan to help you write.

## Writing Plan

**What will the topic of your essay be?**

_____  ◄·►  _____

**What is your opinion on this topic?**

**Reason 1**

_____
_____
_____
_____

◄·►

**Why? Support your reason.**

_____
_____
_____
_____

**Reason 2**

_____
_____
_____
_____

◄·►

**Why? Support your reason.**

_____
_____
_____
_____

**Reason 3**

_____
_____
_____
_____

◄·►

**Why? Support your reason.**

_____
_____
_____
_____

# First Draft

Tips for Writing a Persuasive Essay:

● Grab your reader's attention in the first paragraph.

● State your opinion clearly.

● Support your opinion with clear examples.

● Present your examples from least important to most important.

● Use the last paragraph to summarize your report.

● Use your last paragraph to leave the reader convinced you are right.

## First Draft

**Directions** ⟩ Use your writing plan as a guide for writing your first draft of a *Persuasive Essay*.

_____

_____

_____

_____

_____

_____

_____

_____

_____

_____

_____

_____

_____

_____

*(Continue on your own paper.)*

# Revise the Draft

**Directions** ▷ Use the chart below to help you revise your draft. Check *Yes* or *No* to answer each question in the chart. If you answer *No*, make notes to remind yourself how you can revise, or change, your writing to improve it.

| Question | Yes ✔ | No ✔ | If the answer is no, what will you do to improve your writing? |
|---|---|---|---|
| Do you use your first paragraph to grab the reader's attention? | | | |
| Do you have a clear opinion? | | | |
| Do you include strong reasons that support your opinion? | | | |
| Do you organize your reasons from least to most important? | | | |
| Do you restate your opinion in the last paragraph? | | | |
| Do you use your last paragraph to leave your reader convinced that you are right? | | | |
| Have you corrected mistakes in spelling, grammar, and punctuation? | | | |

**Directions** ▷ Use the notes in your chart and writing plan to revise your draft.

# Writing Report Card

**Directions** ▷ Read your revised draft again or ask someone else to read it. Have the person who reads your paper complete the following Report Card. Revise your paper until you have no less than a Very Good Score for each item.

Title of paper: _____

Purpose of paper: _____ This paper is a persuasive essay. _____

Person who scores the paper: _____

| Score | Writing Goals |
|---|---|
| | Does the writer grab your attention right away? |
| | Is the writer's opinion absolutely clear? |
| | Does the writer include reasons that support his or her opinion? |
| | Are the reasons organized from least to most important? |
| | Does the last paragraph restate the writer's opinion in a new way? |
| | Is the essay convincing? |
| | Are the essay's grammar, spelling, and punctuation correct? |

☺ Excellent Score    ☆ Very Good Score    + Good Score

✔ Acceptable Score    — Needs Improvement

# Writing Skills: Grade 7, Answer Key

Answers to some questions may vary, but examples are provided here to give you an idea of how students may respond. Encourage students to share, discuss, and evaluate their answers, particularly their summaries. Also, encourage students to answer all questions in complete sentences.

**page 22**
1. The first locker law is that tall kids get lockers on the bottom row and short kids get the lockers on top. The second law is that your lock never opens when you're in a hurry. (Make sure that students' answers include details from the story.)
2. The egg salad sandwich law is the third law of lockers. That means whoever brings something stinky like an egg salad sandwich for lunch has the locker above yours. The last locker law is the surprise clean-out. Teachers always know just when you will be most embarrassed by whatever is in your locker and choose that time to call for a clean-out. (Look for a clear understanding of the locker laws in students' answers.)
3. Help students summarize the significant events of the story, paraphrasing as needed. Summaries should be organized in a thoughtful way, with the main ideas and important details clearly presented.

**page 23**
1. The writer uses words like *I, me,* and *mine* to show that this is her personal story.
2. The writer's problem is having a cheerful younger brother who can't wait to start middle school and have a locker.
3. By describing her brother's reactions to each locker law, the writer shows how cheerful and agreeable her brother really is. The writer also uses these reactions to let you know how she feels about her brother.
4. When the writer first describes her brother as amazing, you can almost picture her shaking her head at how goofy she thinks her brother is. In the last paragraph, the writer says her brother is amazing again, but this time, the word *amazing* means something entirely different. The writer sees her brother as loving, optimistic, and eager to start middle school.

**page 30**
1. The writer and his or her family moved to Okinawa for three years.
2. The setting for this story is the island of Okinawa, a place with towering bamboo forests, tall mountains, and houses built next to cemeteries. (Look for an understanding of setting. Help students use vivid, descriptive words that evoke a clear image of the setting.)
3. The first clue the writer had that this experience would be unusual was the summer the family spent in California. They made new friends and spent lots of time at the pool, the movies, and the park.
4. Check to see that students summarize the significant events of the story. Summaries should be organized in a thoughtful way, with the main ideas and important details clearly presented.

**page 31**
1. One way the writer creates an optimistic mood is by using positive descriptions. For example, the writer tells you that the summer was moving up on her list of favorite summers and that the "seriousness of the occasion made people beautiful to watch." The writer also uses humor to help keep the story positive. For example, when the mother opens the refrigerator, the writer says, "That was the last straw, or I should say, roach."
2. The writer ends the paragraph by saying, "You can imagine what I wanted to do to him." The writer knows that anyone who has had something special destroyed knows exactly how the writer felt.
3. The writer uses humor to keep the mood positive. By saying, "...the last straw, or I should say, roach," the writer fits a common saying to their experience.
4. The writer lists all the unusual things that happened during the three years on Okinawa, including holidays for the dead, typhoons, poisonous snakes, roaches, and earthquakes.

# Writing Skills: Grade 7, Answer Key, continued

**page 38**
1. The Bateaux brothers live in Cajun country. A creek with frogs and fish runs behind their house, and an alligator-filled swamp is nearby.
2. Although the writer tells us that one brother's favorite thing is food, the descriptions of Wes and Les as they try to move past the festival food booths and the jambalaya pot convince the readers that the brothers love food. (Encourage students to support their answer with details from the story.)
3. The brothers saw a cook standing on a ladder and stirring jambalaya in a giant black pot. The jambalaya smelled so good that the brothers decided to eat instead of entering their frog in the race. (Encourage students to include specific details from the story.)
4. Guide students in summarizing the significant events of the story. Summaries should be organized in a thoughtful way, with the main ideas and important details clearly presented.

**page 39**
1. The simile is "Both of them looked like soaked muskrats." The metaphor is "Poe shook hard, sending arrows of water in every direction."
2. The writer uses words that are common to the story's setting, making the story more realistic.
3. Pictures will vary but should include a huge pot, an open fire, a cook on a ladder using a canoe paddle to stir the jambalaya, and the Bateaux brothers and Poe.
4. Answers will vary. Answers should be based on what students learned about the Bateaux brothers: they love Poe, the outdoors, and food; and they've been to a fair or festival three weekends in a row. Encourage students to use descriptive words that express all five senses.

**page 46**
1. Dry ice is so cold that it can burn your skin if you touch it. (Check for details from the paper.)
2. Farmers use tiny grains of dust or silver to seed rain clouds. These particles attract water droplets, which combine to form raindrops. (Encourage students to paraphrase information from the paper.)
3. Breathing into the cloud chamber provides enough moisture to form a cloud. After you seed the cloud with dry ice crystals, the moisture from your breath helps the ice crystals grow bigger and eventually fall as snowflakes. (Guide students in paraphrasing the information provided in the paper.)
4. Pictures will vary. Have students discuss how to draw a picture that shows all the parts of the cloud chamber. You may want to suggest a cut-away diagram if students are having trouble drawing and labeling the cloud chamber. Finished diagrams should match the details provided in "Make Your Own Snowstorm."

**page 47**
1. The writer states the purpose of the paper clearly, lists materials, and gives step-by-step instructions.
2. If you are working with a dangerous substance, you need to know how to protect yourself. Since the writer doesn't know if readers are familiar with dry ice, the warning is included to protect them.
3. Listing the materials before giving the directions helps readers make sure they have everything they need before they start making a snowstorm.
4. The writer uses sequence words such as *first, next,* and *then* to help you understand the order of the steps. These words also help you find your place in the process quickly.
5. The last paragraph summarizes the paper, reminds readers that making a snowstorm is a simple process, and challenges them to repeat the experiment.

**page 54**
1. Throughout history, all of these spices were valuable. Salt was pressed into coins more valuable than gold, pepper was reserved for royalty, and saffron was used as a sign of wealth and power. (Check to see that students support their answers with details from the paper.)
2. Answers will vary.
3. How Salt, Pepper, and Saffron Are Alike: Salt, pepper, and saffron are all used to season food.; All three spices have been used as medicines.; Historically, all three spices were very valuable.

How Salt, Pepper, and Saffron Are Different: Salt is found in seawater, salt wells, and underground, while pepper and saffron are harvested from plants.; Salt is white and grainy, and has no scent. Pepper is red, black, or white with a spicy scent. Saffron can be a yellow-orange powder or red threads. It is a fragrant spice.; To obtain salt, people must evaporate seawater, use a salt well to pump up dissolved salt, or mine rock salt and crush it. Pepper starts out as a berry. To create the spice, berries are picked, cleaned, dried, and ground. Saffron comes from the saffron crocus and must be picked by hand. The slender red threads can be sold as is, or ground into a yellow-orange powder.; Although salt and pepper used to be valuable, they seem ordinary today. Saffron, on the other hand, is still very expensive.; In ancient times, salt was used to preserve both food and dead bodies. It was also used as money to pay soldiers in early Rome. While pepper wasn't used as money, it was so expensive that only royalty could have it. Saffron was used as a dye and to make perfumes.

# Writing Skills: Grade 7, Answer Key, continued

**page 55**

1. The writer tells where each spice is found, how the spice is obtained, and each spice's historical uses.
2. By using the same main ideas, the writer makes it easy for readers to identify the similarities and differences among the spices.
3. Salt, pepper, and saffron are precious spices because they are valuable. Salt was once pressed into coins more valuable than gold. Pepper was so expensive that only royalty could have it. Saffron was used as a sign of wealth and power.
4. The first paragraph introduces the topic of the paper. The last paragraph summarizes the main ideas that are presented in the paper.

**page 63**

1. There is no oxygen in a bog, so the bacteria and fungi that break down a body can't live. (Help students incorporate details from the report in their answers.)
2. A glacier is frozen water. Bacteria and fungi need oxygen and liquid water to break down bodies. (Check to see if students included all significant details.)
3. The Ice Man is unusual because he still had his tools, grass cape, bearskin cap, and leather shoes when he was found, about 5,000 years after his death. (Guide students to include details from the report to support their answer.)
4. Guide students in summarizing the report. Summaries should be organized in a thoughtful way, with the main ideas and important details clearly presented.

**page 64**

1. Starting with the fifth paragraph, the paper talks about how people interfere with the decay process.
2. Mentioning the Ice Man in this paragraph lets you know that the Egyptians were preserving their dead about 5,000 years ago.
3. Most people know about the Egyptian mummies. The information in this paragraph tells the readers that mummification was more common than they might have known.
4. The first paragraph introduces the idea of preserved bodies. The last paragraph summarizes what scientists have learned by studying preserved bodies.

**page 71**

1. Jen is writing to the station manager to request more programming that describes the accomplishments of women in air and space. (Guide students in identifying Jen's purpose for writing.)
2. Jen points out that women have played important roles in the history of air and space exploration. She also states that the station could send an important message to school-aged children by showing more programs that include women. Finally, Jen reminds the manager that more than half of the station's viewers are female. (Encourage students to use their own words as they list Jen's reasons for writing.)
3. Television stations make more money when they have large audiences. If over half of the station's viewers are female and they quit watching in protest, the station would lose a lot of money and could possibly go out of business. (Look for a logical conclusion based on the details in the letter.)
4. Guide students in summarizing the reasons Jen gives to the station manager. Summaries should be organized in a thoughtful way, with the main ideas and important details clearly presented.

**page 72**

1. "I've never seen a single program that describes the accomplishments of women in air and space."
2. Jen provides several specific examples of women who played important roles in the history of flight. This shows the station manager that the information is readily available and important.
3. Answers will vary. Be sure that students base their conclusions on information that is provided in the letter.
4. By adding this title, Jen shows the station manager that she is serious about working in space someday. Seeing programs that feature the contributions of women in air and space could inspire her to make important contributions herself.

# Writing Skills: Grade 7, Answer Key, continued

**page 79**

1. The important characters in *To Kill a Mockingbird* are Scout, Jem, Boo Radley, Atticus, and Tom Robinson.
2. The writer describes the struggle between people, especially black and white people in the South. Another struggle the writer talks about is the one between tolerance and prejudice. (Help students identify details from the review.)
3. There are several opposites in the movie *To Kill a Mockingbird.* They include love and hate, truth and lies, fear and bravery, and right and wrong. The movie also shows how people are and how they can be. (Guide students to restate the information found in the review.)
4. Check to see that students identify the purpose of the review and summarize its significant points. Summaries should be organized in a thoughtful way, with the main reasons for seeing the movie and the important details clearly presented.

**page 80**

1. Most movies today are not only in color, but they also have lots of special effects. If the movie is black and white, you might think the movie is so old that you don't want to watch it.
2. Scout, one of Atticus's children, is the narrator of the movie, so the story is told the way the children see it.
3. By mentioning the awards that the book and movie received, the writer is telling the reader that he or she is not the only person who thinks this movie is great.
4. In the first paragraph, the writer states his or her opinion that everyone should read *To Kill a Mockingbird* and then see the movie. The writer restates this opinion in the last paragraph by telling the reader about the awards won by the book and the movie. The last paragraph also summarizes the reasons that everyone should see the movie.

**page 87**

1. Many people are terrified of speaking in front of a group. Taking a speech class gives you practice in public speaking and makes you more confident. (Encourage students to paraphrase the information from the essay.)
2. The writer says that being confident means that you can talk without shaking in a language that sounds like English to classmates who listen because you know what you're talking about. (Guide students to include all significant details.)
3. The first thing you learn is to think before you speak.
4. Check to see that students identify the purpose of the essay and summarize its significant points. Summaries should be organized in a thoughtful way, with the main reasons for taking a speech class and the important details clearly presented.

**page 88**

1. The writer uses humor in the first paragraph to capture your attention. The exaggerated questions remind you of your worst experience in front of the class and make you laugh at yourself.
2. The writer uses humor to show that everyone is in the same position. Very few people like speaking in front of a group. If you can laugh at yourself, you'll be more open to learning a new skill.
3. If you decide to "wing it" for your speech, you will experience some of the same things the writer describes in the first paragraph. The writer directs your attention to the first paragraph to point out that this is not a good strategy.
4. The first paragraph describes how you might feel if you have never taken a speech class. The last paragraph demonstrates how different the experience can be if you have taken a speech class and are prepared.